Basics of
Ship
Modeling

The
Illustrated
Guide

Mike Ashey

KALMBACH
BOOKS

DEDICATION:
Joel and Marion Swanson

Printed in the United States of America

06 07 08 09 10 11 12 13 14 15   10 9 8 7 6 5 4 3 2

Visit our Web site at http://kalmbachbooks.com
Secure online ordering available

Publisher's Cataloging in Publication
(Provided by Quality Books, Inc.)

Ashey, Mike.
Basics of ship modeling: the illustrated guide
/ Mike Ashey. — 1st ed.
p. cm.
Includes index.
ISBN: 0-89024-372-7

I. Ship models. I. Title.

VM298.A84 2000   623.8'201
QBI99-1906

ISBN-10: 0-89024-372-7
ISBN-13: 978-0-89024-372-5

Book design: Jonathan Johnson
Cover design: Kristi Ludwig

Cover: 1/350 scale Classic Warships *USS Miami,* built by Mike Ashey
Photo by Jim Forbes

ACKNOWLEDGMENTS: Many people have helped me over the years and have in many ways, directly and indirectly, contributed to this book. Special thanks are due to Dr. Eric Lubot, Dr. Randy Frosstrum, and Dr. Mia Anderson of Bergen Community College, Paramus, New Jersey; Dr. Ray McAllister, Professor Emeritus of Ocean Engineering, Florida Atlantic University; The Hobby Caboose of Tallahassee, Florida, and the Big Bend Scale Modelers Club; Glenn Johnson for his photography work; Scott Weller, Richard Boutin Sr., and Bill Teehan of Tallahassee, Florida; Al Ross of Bangor, Maine; Randy Chisum of Bryan, Texas; Kelly Quirk of Liberty, Missouri; and Chris Preston of Victoria, British Columbia, for allowing me to showcase their models in this book; Terry Spohn of Kalmbach Publishing; Joel and Marian Swanson for their encouragement; my parents, Joseph and Marie, for instilling within me an engine that knows no rest; and, most important, special thanks are due to my sons, Thomas and Gregory, for giving me some space to get the book done, and my wife, Kelly, for helping me every step of the way.

All color photos are by Glenn Johnson of Glenn Johnson Photoillustration of Tallahassee, Florida, unless otherwise noted. All black-and-white photos are by the author unless otherwise noted.

Contents

Foreword

I wrote *Basics of Ship Modeling: The Illustrated Guide* in an effort to show modelers by means of step-by-step pictures how to create detailed, realistic-appearing scale ship models. Although each chapter is designed to provide as much information as possible, some sections of this book can be used in conjunction with my first book, *Building and Detailing Scale Model Ships* (Kalmbach Publishing Co.), while other sections deal with entirely new subjects. This book shows you how to build flawless plastic and resin ship models from start to finish; remove seams and cure fit problems; work with resin kits and fix resin casting problems with simple solutions; drill out portholes; add hatches and chains; drill out gun barrels; work with brass and stainless steel photoetching and build up complicated photoetched parts; mask and paint, apply decals, and add weathering; and scratchbuild and detail superstructure parts.

Since modelers create three-dimensional objects, and much of the modeling process requires visual interpretation, the majority of us in this hobby fall into the category of visual people; we respond well to visual stimuli. This book capitalizes on our visual sense by presenting pictures in place of words. While words are also valuable, it can take an entire page of text to describe just one picture. Since my motivation for writing this book was to pack as much information as I could into a limited number of pages, the best way to do this is to convey ideas, techniques, procedures, and successes through pictures.

I think I have accomplished what I set out to do. Always remember that the true nature of this hobby is creating scale models by exploring and expanding the boundaries of your abilities and imagination and most of all—having fun!

Happy modeling,
Mike Ashey

Chapter One

Building Plastic Kits

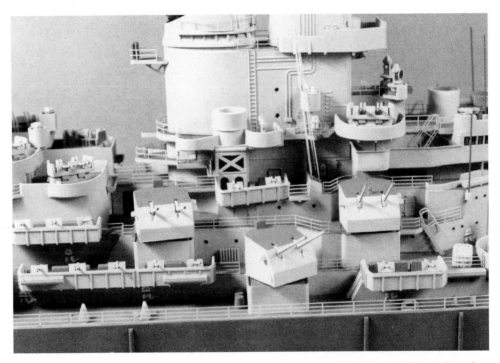

1/350 scale *USS Missouri* built by Mike Ashey

To have a successful experience building plastic ship kits it's important to study the instructions first and become familiar with all the parts and assembly sequences. I spend a lot of time test-fitting the hull, deck, and superstructure parts to find out where the fit problems are so I can decide how best to deal with them. Every ship kit is different and each one, no matter who the manufacturer is, has its own unique fit problems and minor flaws. Sometimes the decks do not exactly butt up against the sides of the hull, and there may be a slight gap to fill. Sometimes main deck sections do not line up correctly, or there may be a space between sections, or a superstructure level might sit skewed. Whatever the problem, there is always a simple solution.

I like to keep my workbench neat and organized. Since ship kits can have a lot of parts and subassemblies, I use plastic storage boxes for organizing them. These lidded bin organizers are usually found in the sewing sections of arts and crafts stores. They are great for organizing the parts you will be working with—not to mention the fact that you will be a lot less likely to lose any parts if they are all stored in one place.

Once I get set up, I decide how I will display the model and then begin making the necessary modifications to the hull. At this point I pick out the piece of wood I want to use for the display base, cut it to size, and stain it. I decide what color scheme I want and assemble the paints and mix the colors, test them, and make any adjustments that are needed. I also decide how I will assemble the kit, since I use the instructions only as a general guide. This is an important point because the assembly sequence you follow will depend on the display you choose, the color scheme, details you may want to add, changes you may want to make to the kit, and how you want to deal with any problems you have identified.

When removing parts from trees, be careful how you cut them off. This is the first step in dealing with seam removal. If you snap off the parts you will most likely damage them, which means either repair work to the part or extra work to fill a seam.

Next, check each part for a casting line and carefully scrape off this line with the edge of a number 11 X-acto blade. For parts that will be glued together, check the gluing surfaces. You will almost always find small injection marks that you'll have to flatten. Check the fit of these assemblies—the locating pins are not always correct.

Sometimes you can get a better fit by removing the pins and running the part halves across a stationary piece of sandpaper to flatten the gluing surfaces. Sometimes the surfaces of parts have small,

round indentations. Typically, you will not find these round indentations in newer kits, but older kits produced in the early years of plastic modeling can have a lot of them. The indentations result from the injection-molding process, and there are several ways to get rid of them. You can fill them by punching out a thin plastic disk using a Waldron punch tool, gluing it in the hole, and sanding it smooth, or you can hide them if sanding them will destroy detail.

When you check the fit of superstructure parts on deck surfaces, or when you have to stack superstructure layers, you will almost always find voids around the bases of each layer. The secret to dealing

Use a pair of wire cutters to cut the trees connected to the parts. Then you can do the fine trim work with a number 11 X-acto blade.

with these is to fill them with white glue applied with a thin wire applicator and then remove the excess with a damp cotton swab.

As you build up the superstructure, I recommend that you cut and measure photoetched railings and then set them aside until you are ready to use them. In some cases you may have to add photoetched railings and ladders as you build up the superstructure, because they may be impossible to add later on. Here again, a little planning is important because it will make assembly a lot easier.

Sometimes filling voids on superstructure assemblies cannot be accomplished with white glue because the gap is too wide. In these cases, I use small sections of Evergreen strip, half-round, and quarter-round plastic to hide the voids.

Another trick is to use Evergreen half rounds to cover seams and gaps where two prepainted superstructure parts meet and form a flat surface.

Sometimes you'll have to reinforce fragile superstructure parts so they will not break when you are fixing the seams or adding detail. I use small lengths of Evergreen strips glued to the inside of the parts. Another trick I use to help glue large superstructure parts to the deck is to fill the inside of the part with resin. This gives me a large gluing surface on the underside. I can glue it down without having to run a bead of glue around the base of the superstructure where it meets the deck, which can mar the deck surface.

The decks of large scale kits may flex slightly once they are glued to the hull. This sometimes occurs because the span between the sides of the hull is wide and the plastic deck is too thin. To prevent this flexing, simply glue sections of thick Evergreen strips to the underside of the deck, but be sure these strips do not interfere with the deck-to-hull fit, or any parts that may be attached to the deck.

Typically, I assemble the hull, insert the display pedestals into their locations, glue down the deck, and then add the shafts, struts, and rudder. I then prime and paint the hull and main deck, add the props, and finally attach the model to the display base.

At this point I set the completed hull aside and start assembling the superstructure parts, fixing flaws, filling seams, smoothing out surfaces, adding detail, measuring photoetched railings and ladders, and painting the parts. I then build up the superstructure, adding photoetched railings when necessary. I also add the masts at this point. Then I turn my attention to fittings like searchlights, gun directors, radars, boats and davits, cranes, and catapults. Finally, I assemble all the large and small caliber guns, paint and install them, and then add the rigging.

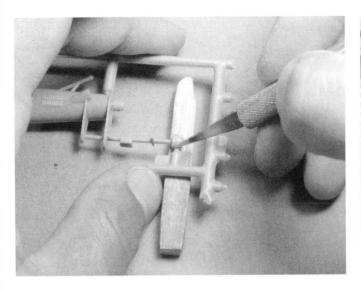

To trim delicate parts from their trees, place a piece of balsa under the part and then cut it with a number 11 X-acto blade.

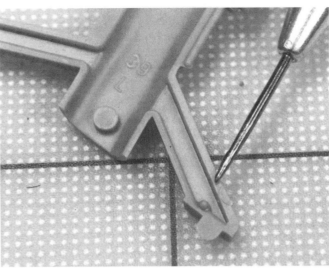

Prior to gluing together part halves check the gluing surfaces for raised mold lines. Carefully scrape off these mold lines with a number 11 X-acto blade.

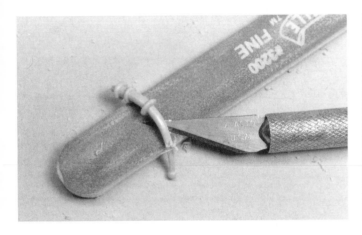

To remove the mold lines from small parts carefully scrape them off with the tip of a number 11 X-acto blade.

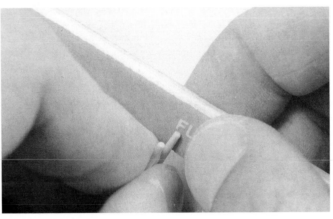

Use a Flex-I-File sanding stick to help reshape parts after you scrape off the mold lines.

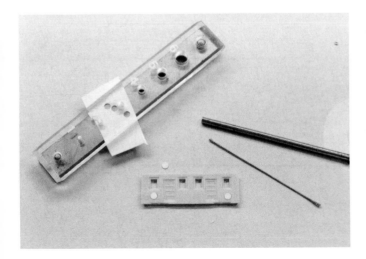

Waldron Products punch tool is great for fixing indented injection marks. Select the disk size closest to the indentation. Glue the disk into place with super glue and then carefully sand the disk to blend into the surface.

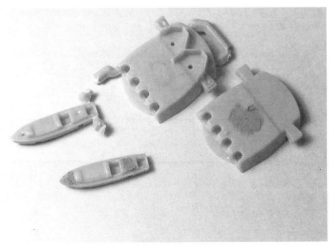

Although dimples are easy to fix with super glue, you can also use putty.

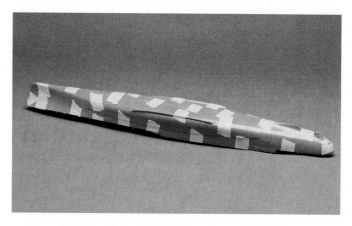

Always test-fit the hull and deck parts to ensure that they fit together before gluing. This will allow you to figure out how to fix any problems.

To glue the hull together, run a bead of super glue on both the inside and the outside of the hull along the seam line. I like to use a .5mm lead pencil or a length of stiff brass wire to apply the glue.

Testors silver paint makes an excellent seam, crack, and flaw detector. After the paint dries, simply apply more super glue to any flawed areas. Remove the paint with Polly-S Paint and Decal Remover and then sand the super glue.

To add strength to a multiple-piece hull, glue lengths of Evergreen strip stock along the inside of the hull along the seam line.

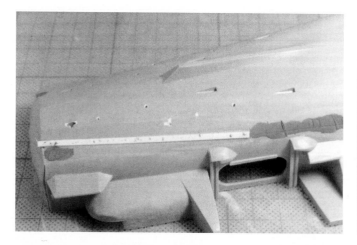

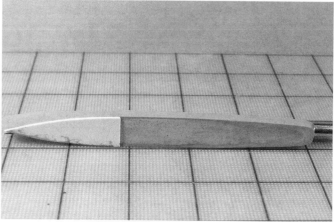

To fill seam lines on the exterior of the hull, you can use putty or thin lengths of Evergreen plastic strip. If you use the Evergreen strip be sure that the plastic strip is completely covered with super glue before applying it to the hull.

To increase the gluing surface on this 1/700 scale hull, pour resin into the hull. Add evergreen plastic sheet to the forward section of the hull. Then, when it's placed on the diorama base, the ship will be more realistic.

To reinforce brass pedestals, stack glued sheets of Evergreen plastic to the inside of the hull and then drill them out.

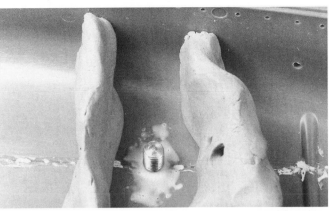

Another method is to glue the pedestal into place with white glue and then carefully build a box around the top of the pedestal inside the hull with clay.

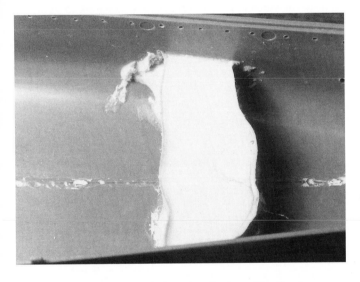

The next step is to pour resin into the clay box. After it sets, super glue the edges of the resin to the interior of the hull, because resin won't adhere to plastic.

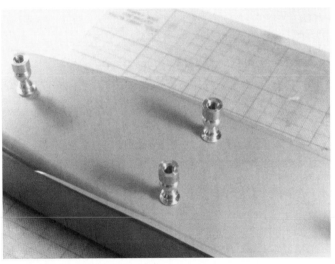

These brass pedestals are nothing more than lamp finials that you can find in a local hardware or lamp store. They are turned brass with one end having a long stem screw and the other end set up for screw insertion.

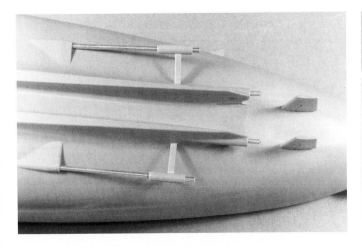

I like to use brass rod for propeller shaft applications whenever it's feasible. Here, Tamiya's *Missouri* sports new brass rod propeller shafts.

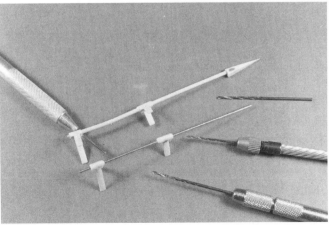

To fix warped one-piece shafts and struts, cut the shafts from the V struts and carefully drill out the struts to the diameter of the brass rod you select for the shafts. When drilling, start with a small bit and work up to the bit size that you need for the brass rod.

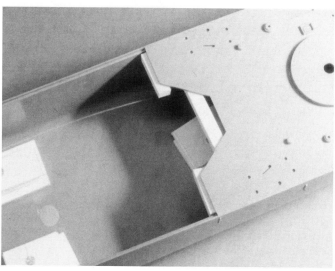

Position the V struts with the brass rods in place. Glue the struts to the hull and then remove the brass rods. The hull is now ready for painting.

To help strengthen main deck connections, glue thick strips of Evergreen strip stock to the underside of the deck.

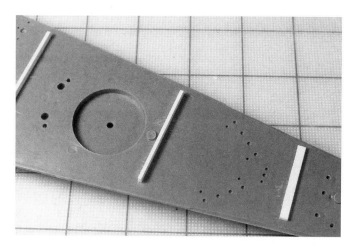

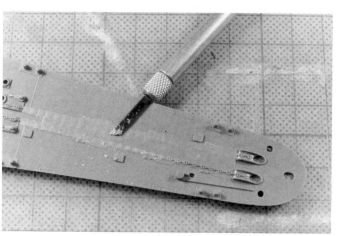

To help reinforce and strengthen decks, you can glue strips of Evergreen to the underside of the deck. Be careful that the strips do not interfere with parts placement or with the hull/deck connection.

To remove molded-on chains, carefully scrape them off using an X-acto stencil knife.

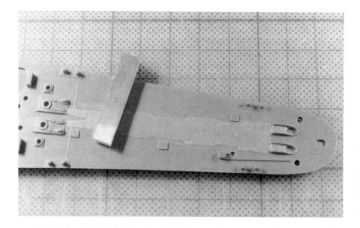

To smooth out the surface, cut a small piece off a Flex-I-File sanding stick and carefully wet-sand the surface.

To fix any gouges, carefully apply automotive scratch filler putty with the stencil knife tip, and then wet-sand smooth with a Flex-I-File sanding stick after it dries.

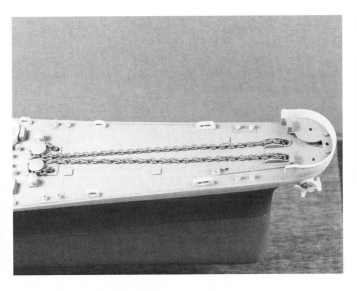

Removing the molded chains from Tamiya's *USS Missouri* and replacing them with real chains adds realism. Don't forget to drill out holes where the chains go into the deck.

Use Testors putty to fill voids between the deck edge and the hull. I like to scrape the putty flat prior to sanding it smooth.

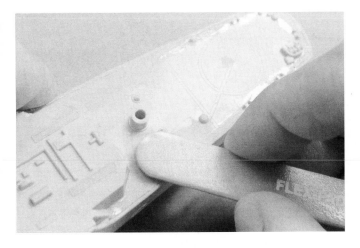

To smooth the filler between the deck and the hull on Monogram's *USS Halsey,* I wet-sanded the area with a Flex-I-File sanding stick. To fill the voids between the deck and hull on this kit, I used super glue instead of putty.

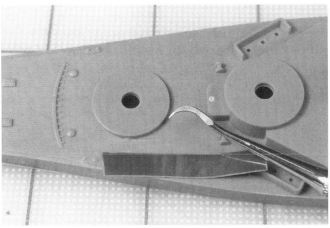

To repair deck detail, use labeling tape as a guide and use a Bare Metal Foil plastic scriber to rescribe and connect the wood deck lines.

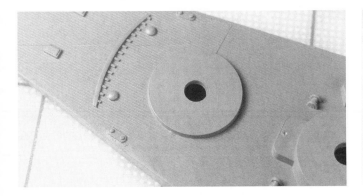

The port side deck surface on this 1/700 scale kit has been re-scribed. Once the deck is painted it will be hard to tell the difference between the indented scribed lines and the raised scribed lines. Aircraft modelers use this same trick all the time to replace raised panel lines on aircraft surfaces.

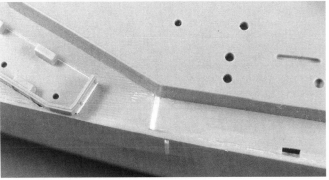

To fix gaps between adjoining deck surfaces carefully glue a strip of Evergreen plastic between the connection points.

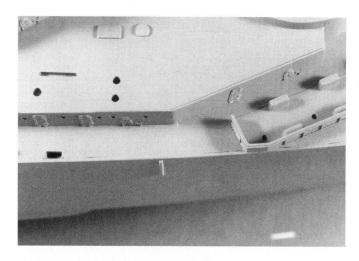

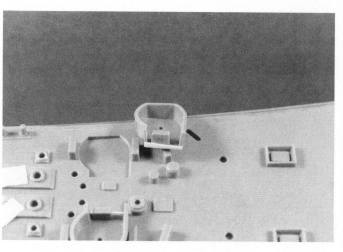

Sand the gap smooth and re-scribe the deck. On this kit I left the voids at the junction point between the deck and the hull because the brass railings would cover the area.

To fix gaps in parts that insert into the deck, simply glue a strip of plastic in the location of the gap and carefully form-fit it into place.

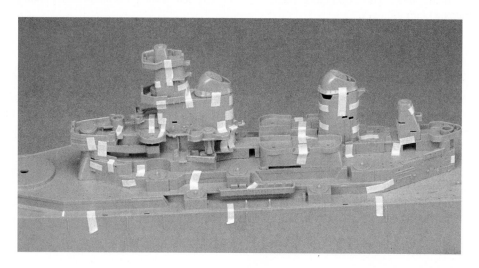

Tape together the superstructure parts. Then connect all the parts and place them on the hull. Note any fit problems and voids so that you can figure out what approach to take to fix them. Photo by Glenn Johnson

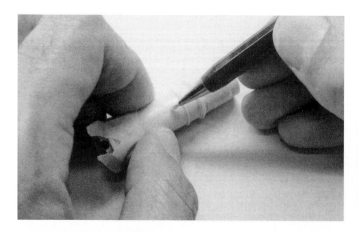

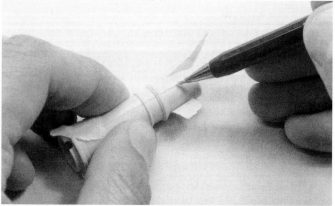

To glue together parts, especially superstructure parts, position the parts, tape them together tightly, and run a bead of thin super glue along the seam between the tape. The capillary action of the super glue will cause the glue to seep into the mating surfaces of the parts.

After the glue is dry, remove the masking tape and finish applying glue along the seam line.

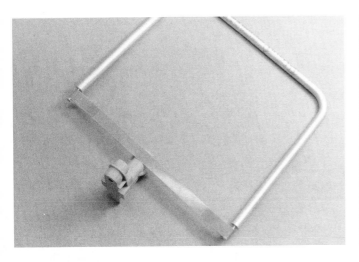

Once the glue is dry, carefully scrape and sand the super glue bead line so that it blends into the surface. For curved surfaces use a Flex-I-File to maintain the contours of the part.

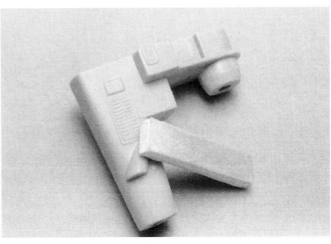

Use small lengths of Flex-I-File sanding sticks to get into corner areas. They are also great for removing unwanted molded-on detail.

One way to deal with injection marks that are impossible to reach is to hide them. Thin mesh screening punched out with a Waldron punch tool covers the injection marks on this part.

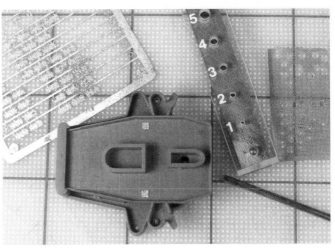

Another way to hide blemishes or imperfections is to cover them with Gold Medal Models deck hatches.

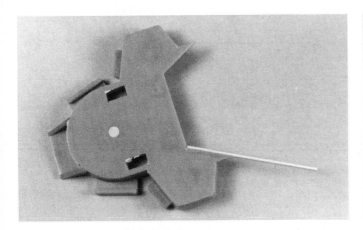

Fix voids between superstructure parts by adding thin strips of Evergreen stock to the gluing surfaces and then form-fitting them into place.

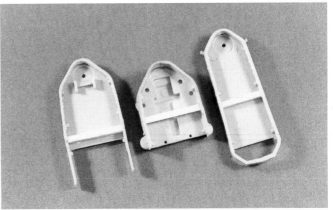

To reinforce flimsy superstructure parts, glue them together and then add strips of Evergreen strip stock to the inside of the parts. Be careful when doing this—you don't want to distort the shape of the part. Kit parts by Bill Teehan

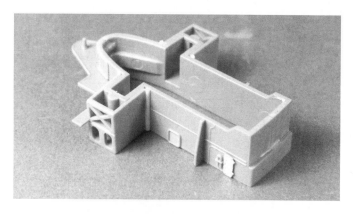

Interior corner joints can be difficult to fill. An easier way to deal with these problems is to simply cover them with small lengths of Evergreen quarter-round stock.

When fixing seams, surround the area with tape to protect surface detail. Fill a seam line with automotive crack filler and wet-sand it smooth with a small length of a Flex-I-File sanding stick. This area is now ready for painting.

Next, prime the area, and add a Gold Medal Models photoetched detail fire hose. It is now ready for final painting.

Exterior corner joints can be a challenge to fill and then smooth out, but automotive scratch filler makes it easy. While you can't use this scratch filler for large voids, it works well for small, thin crack lines and voids, and it sands quickly. Here again, use a small length of a Flex-I-File sanding stick to smooth out the putty.

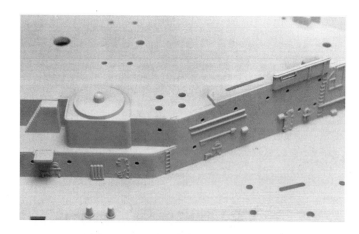

Here you can see that the putty has completely filled the areas. After applying primer, you cannot detect the cracks.

Some superstructures require a lot of fill work, like Monogram's age-old *USS Halsey.* Here, apply combinations of Evergreen strip stock and thin- and thick-gel super glue to the seams and voids. The trick is to carefully sand these surfaces smooth while retaining the shape of the superstructure parts. Using small lengths of Flex-I-File sanding sticks is the best way to do this.

After cleaning up, reshaping, and adding brass details, railings, and ladders, the superstructure of Monogram's *USS Halsey* is ready for painting. Replace the bridge windows with Gold Medal Models bridge window decals. Photo by Glenn Johnson

One way to add porthole details is to use a thin length of labeling tape positioned along the superstructure surface. Use a needle point inserted into a pin vise to mark the locations of the portholes, and then drill them out.

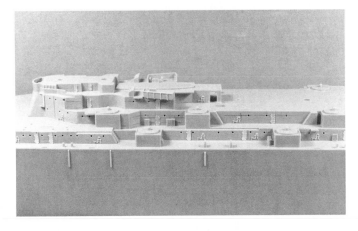

Here is a good example of adding details to a superstructure. While Tamiya's 1/350 scale *Missouri* is a great kit, adding Gold Medal Models hatches and fire hoses, as well as locating and drilling out portholes, is a great way to add a higher level of realism. A twist drill is a handy piece of equipment to have when you're drilling out a lot of portholes.

You can improve even 1/700 scale superstructure parts by adding photoetched details and drilling out portholes.

To fill voids between the superstructure and the deck, apply white glue. Work in small sections at a time so that the glue doesn't start to dry before you shape it.

To shape white glue, simply dampen a cotton swab in your mouth, twirling it to compress the cotton, then run the tip along the edge of the superstructure and the deck, thereby removing the excess glue and pushing the glue down into the void.

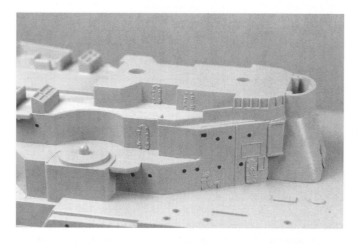

Fill the deck/superstructure seams on Tamiya's 1/350 scale *Missouri* and prime the model. While white glue is not the answer to all void problems, it is by far the best filler to use for voids between superstructures and decks.

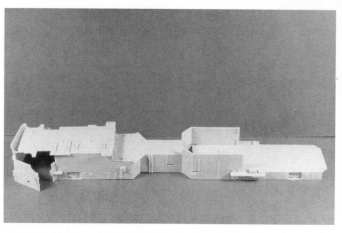

The superstructure parts on DML's 1/350 scale kits present a special challenge to modelers because they are not designed as left and right halves; you literally have to build a five-part box—four sides and a top. The secret is to start from the stern portion of the main superstructure and work forward. The stern parts are easier to fit together.

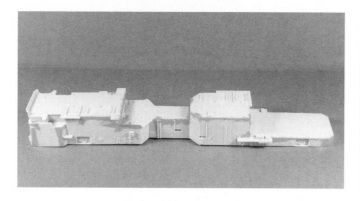

Complete the DML superstructure and apply silver paint to the seams to check for flaws. You have to be careful when sanding the corner areas on this particular kit because you don't want to skew the sharp edges of the superstructure.

Build up superstructures in sections wherever possible, especially with kits that have multiple levels. Here, some of the superstructure parts on Tamiya's 1/350 scale *Missouri* have been completed and are ready for painting.

Build up complex superstructures in stages. Here, the buildup of Tamiya's 1/350 scale *Missouri* has begun.

The stern area of the *Missouri's* superstructure is complete. Now work on the forward section, one layer at a time.

The forward superstructure is now complete. As you build up the superstructure, prepaint all the subassemblies. Use white glue to fill the tiny voids between the deck layers. Because white glue dries clear and transmits light as well as color, it is not necessary to paint the white glue where the parts are already painted. The glue transmits the color of the deck and superstructure.

Sometimes, because of the engineering of a kit and the assembly sequence, you can't always fix a flat surface seam (center of photo, one-fourth up from bottom) prior to painting. In these cases you have three choices: You can live with the seam. You can fill it carefully, sand it, and then repaint the surface—which can be difficult and time-consuming. A better way is to hide it.

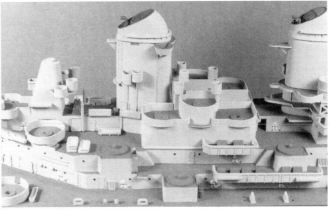

Covering a seam with a small length of prepainted Evergreen half-round stock is not 100 percent accurate. But it's better than leaving the seam there or taking the chance of ruining surface detail by trying to fill it.

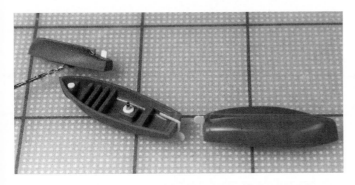

Adding details such as rudders and small smoke stacks to personnel boats adds another level of realism as well as helping to cover flaws.

Adding boat straps to this 1/500 scale kit gives yet another layer of realism. Model by Scott Weller

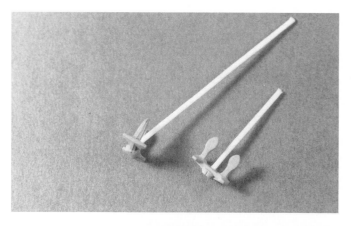

You'll have to replace the center stems on anchors on most ship kits so the anchors will sit correctly against the hulls.

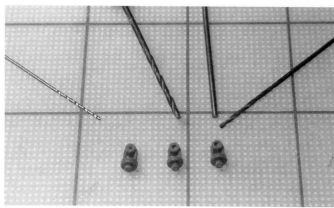

Drilling out the lenses on searchlights is a quick and easy way to add detail to these parts. The final drill bit size that you use should match a Waldron punch disk size.

The search lights on Heller's *Jean Bart* were drilled out and replaced with clear disk parts punched out with a Waldron punch disk set.

Here is another good example of searchlight detail. Revell's popular 1/426 scale *Arizona* looks a lot better with drilled out searchlights as well as photoetched railings.

Sometimes a good paint job on a searchlight will also work, especially if the searchlight has a curved surface, which would be hard to simulate with a clear disk.

Little bits and pieces can also add detail to other parts like cranes. On Revell's *USS Arizona,* for instance, remove some of the molded-on detail and add photoetched detail, as well as new crane hooks.

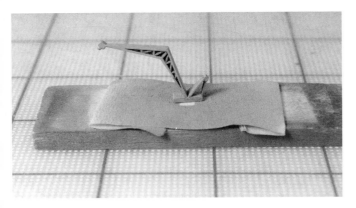

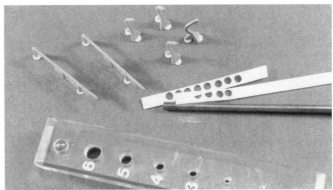

For small-scale cranes you can paint the areas between the lattice-work, which will improve their appearance. A better solution would be to replace this part with a photoetched crane.

Another problem is that small detail parts do not always fit into their deck locations correctly. This becomes an acute problem when the deck is already painted. A simple solution is to add small thin disks to the base of these parts.

Glued to the deck surface of Tamiya's *Missouri*, the part covers the holes that would have resulted from misalignment. It was impossible to fill the void around the base of the 20mm splinter shield. Instead, I carefully filled the void with white glue and left it unpainted.

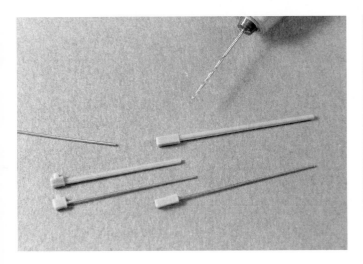

Molded antennas are usually too thick so I like to replace them with lengths of brass wire. Simply cut them off their bases, drill a hole into the base, and glue the brass rod in place.

Adding parts to gun directors and range finders adds detail to them. Here again, you can hide flaws that are hard to fix.

All the small details you add to the superstructure, as well as the small parts, add realism and give the model a very busy-looking appearance.

The appearance of jet aircraft can be greatly improved by just carefully drilling out the intake and exhaust areas of the engines.

The appearance of propeller aircraft can be greatly improved with the addition of photoetched propellers, wheels, and tailhooks.

Add wheels to 1/700 scale planes like these by punching out small disks with a Waldron punch tool.

The biplanes on Revell's USS Arizona have solid wing struts. Cut the struts off and replace them with thin-diameter brass rod. These aircraft look a lot more realistic with these struts. The struts plus a good paint job really improve the overall appearance of this kit.

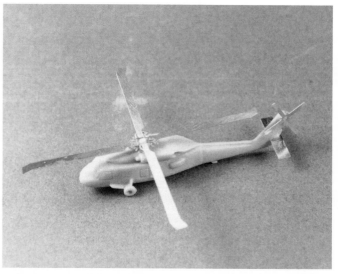

Improve the appearance of helicopters as well by adding photo-etched detail parts.

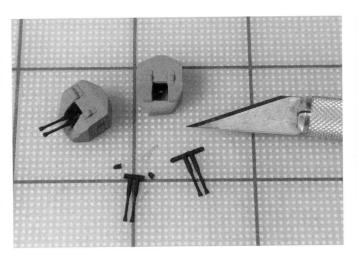

Don't add the guns to these 1/400 scale parts until you have assembled the gun turret, filled the seams, and reshaped the turret. This is a good example of modifying the kit assembly sequence to fix seam problems.

Fill the gun turrets with white glue to simulate the blast bags and to hide the lack of detail inside the turrets.

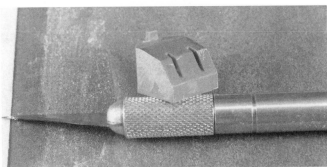

Tamiya's 1/350 scale twin 5-inch mounts have separate side plates. When glued together, they create seams that are almost impossible to fix. The solution is to glue the parts together and then carefully cut off the range finder appendages.

The next step is to fill the seams with super glue and carefully scrape, sand, and smooth the surfaces.

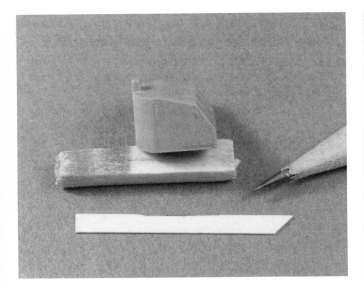

The first step in replacing the detail is to mark the locations of these parts.

To replace the access hatch detail on the forward portion of the turrets, you can create the parts using Evergreen strip stock and your chopper.

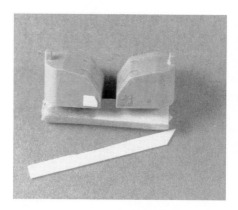

The left turret has an access hatch made from strip stock, while the right turret has a custom-made photoetched hatch.

At this point you can glue the range finder appendages back onto the sides of the turret.

Add hatches to the rear turrets after marking the locations.

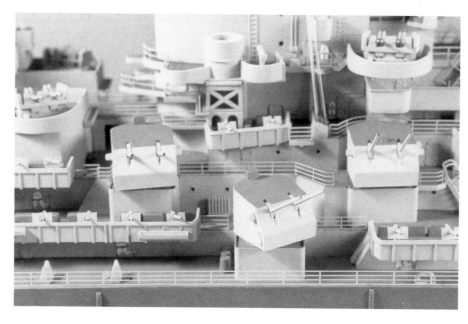

Paint the completed twin 5-inch turrets and install them.

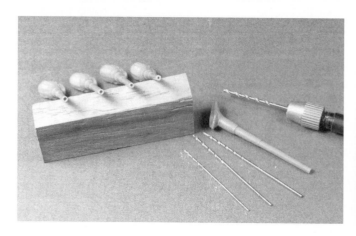

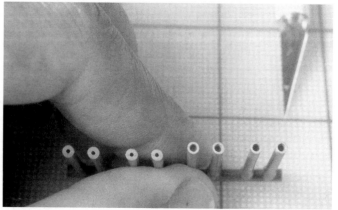

One way to bore out gun barrels is to start with a small drill bit and work up to the largest size drill bit you wish to use. The trick is to center punch the barrel so that your drill bit will not skew to one side.

If you don't have the right size drill bit you can also use the tip of a number 11 X-acto blade to enlarge the hole.

The main turret guns on modern U.S. battleships have independent elevating gun barrels. Simulating this detail adds another level of realism.

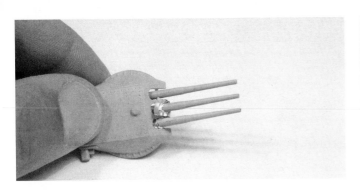

To create blast bags, place aluminum foil at the base of the gun barrels and tuck the aluminum foil underneath the face of the gun turret.

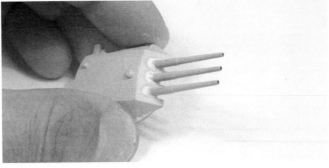

To simulate the blast bags, add white glue to the face of the aluminum foil, being careful not to allow the glue to spill out onto the turret face.

Then paint the finished turrets and paint the blast bags black.

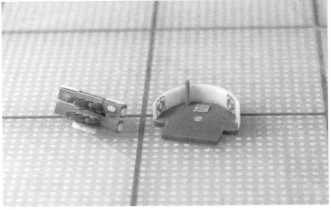

Add parts to the 1/400 scale pom pom gun, as well as the gun platform, to enhance the overall appearance of the gun. Replace the splinter shield with a section of Evergreen plastic tubing, as well.

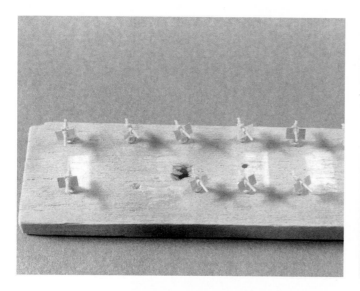

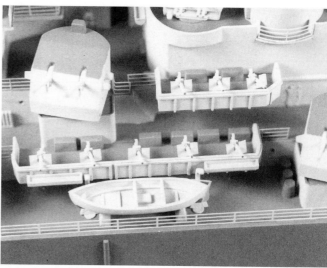

Parts control is important for ship modeling, especially when you are dealing with hundreds of parts. Photoetched shields were added to these 1/350 scale 20mm guns. They are now ready to be painted.

When installing 20mm guns, be sure that the guns are straight and level, especially with respect to each other and the splinter shields that surround them.

To help assemble Tamiya's 40mm gun shields use a small length of Evergreen strip stock to balance the upper part while you glue it into place.

Enhance 1/350 scale 40mm guns like these with railings and gunsights from Gold Medal Models.

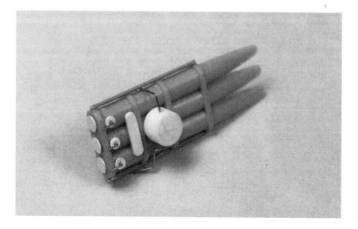

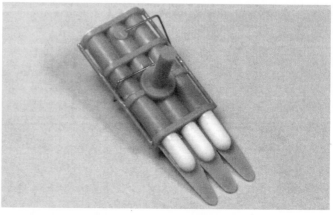

You can enhance torpedo tubes in 1/500 scale and larger with disks, lengths of brass wire, and other scratchbuilt shapes.

To really enhance the appearance of torpedo tubes, add the torpedoes to the underside of the tubes.

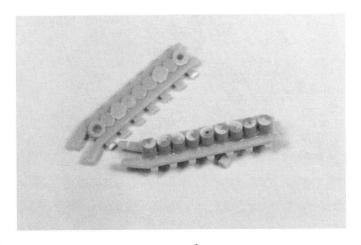

Enhance the appearance of this depth charge rack by adding small lengths of plastic rod to increase the size of the individual depth charges.

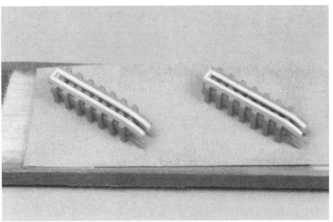

Add small lengths of Evergreen strip stock to these depth charge racks to cover the gluing surfaces that resulted from adding the individual depth charges.

On 1/700 scale kits I recommend you buy a good supply of Pit-Road detail sets to replace kit-supplied parts. These sets, especially the guns, are highly detailed and impressive.

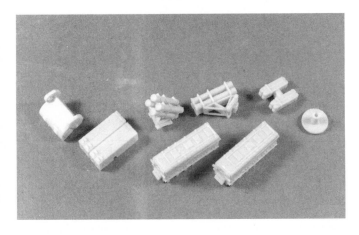

Build up modern weapons sets in stages, just as you would with superstructure parts.

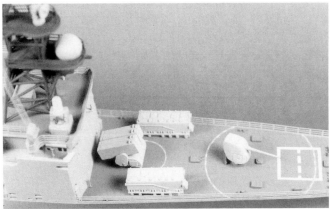

Modern missile systems are very different from their early predecessors and are usually box-shaped in appearance.

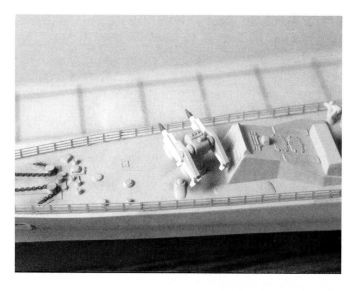

Enhance the appearance of earlier missile systems by rotating the missile arms upward and carefully painting the parts.

Careful painting on this Phalanx Gatling gun helps bring out the detail on this part.

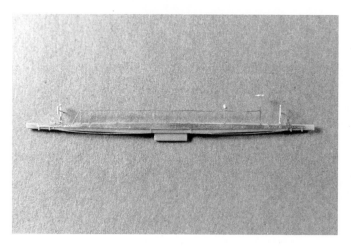

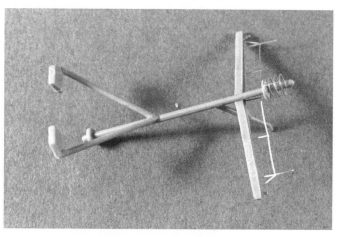

To enhance the detail of Tamiya's main mast for the *Missouri,* glue a Gold Medal Models photoetched mast yardarm to the back side of the kit part.

This is another good example of using a photoetched yardarm bent to shape and glued to the kit-supplied mast.

To add strength to kit-supplied masts, drill out the base of the mast and insert a small length of brass rod.

Wherever possible build up masts in subassemblies. I glued together these four 1/700 scale mast parts and added photo-etched railings prior to painting.

The masts on Heller's 1/400 scale *Jean Bart* have been painted and glued into place and are now ready for rigging.

The starboard side of this lattice structure mast is too wide. Since the superstructure and the mast have been painted, this fit problem requires a unique solution.

To fix this problem, cut the bottom frame so that you can pinch the starboard side of the base of the mast inward.

Pinch the mast base inward, glue it together with super glue, and paint it over. The dissected part is barely noticeable.

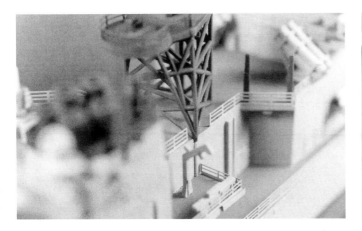

As you can see, the base of the mast fits snugly into its superstructure location after reinstallation. While this glaring problem should have been caught during the fitting phase, it had a simple solution.

In preparation for rigging, drill holes into the flag bags before assembling the superstructure completely. This is a good example of planning—it would have been very difficult to drill these holes after assembling the superstructure.

Rig the forward mast and flag bag with clear nylon sewing thread; paint the thread after installation. To ensure that the rigging is evenly spaced on the mast, install one length on the port side, then install its counterpart on the starboard side, and work your way from the inside of the mast to the outward edge of the mast.

If you are going to add flags to your rigging, curl them slightly so that they appear to be flapping in the breeze.

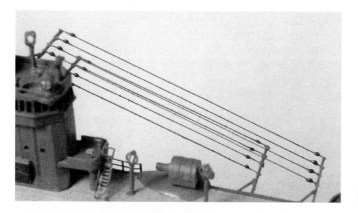

If you want to add the insulators to antenna rigging, simulate the insulators with small drops of white glue. Model by Scott Weller

To keep yardarms from sagging down when you add flag bag rigging, add rigging between the yardarm and the upper part of the mast.

When rigging 1/700 scale kits use nylon thread, but don't paint it. In this scale you should see a hint of rigging, but the rigging should not overwhelm the appearance of the model.

Chapter Two

Building Resin Kits

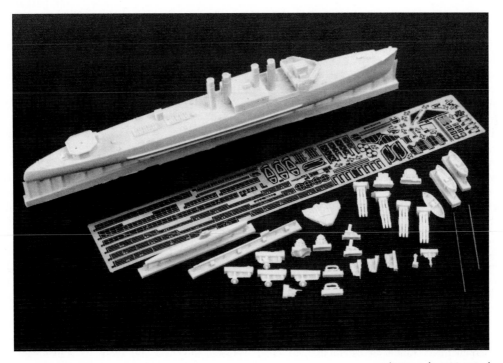

1/350 scale *USS Ward*

Over the past few years there has been an explosion in the variety and scale of resin ship kits. These kits are manufactured very differently from injection-molded kits in a process that is quite labor-intensive. The first step is to scratchbuild a set of masters from materials such as basswood, plastic, and brass. The designer of the master patterns must create the parts, engineer how they will fit together and how they will be cast, and decide whether resin or white metal will be used. Once the master patterns are complete, a set of molds are made from liquid RTV rubber. The molds are specifically engineered for the master pattern parts, and this can be a very intensive trial-and-error process. Once the molds are complete, a set of castings are made to see if any changes are needed. If adjustments to either the master patterns or the molds are necessary, new molds must be created.

Once the designer is satisfied with the master patterns and the resulting casting, photoetching is designed for the kit. A test run of the photoetching is done and individual parts are test-fitted to the castings. If adjustments are needed, the drawings are modified and then the photoetched design is certified for completion. The last step is to write a set of instructions that includes either pictures or drawings. The kits are then mass-produced, packaged, and marketed. There is no automation in the mold-making or casting process; it is all done manually, which adds a great deal to the overall price of the kit. In addition, mold-making and casting is usually done using a pressure chamber or vacuum chamber, which adds to the time, effort, and expense required to produce a kit. Finally, the RTV molds last for only 50 or fewer castings, so new molds must be redone often. Now you know why they cost so much.

Typically, when you open the box of a resin kit you will find that the hull, which is solid resin, is wrapped in bubble pack, while superstructure parts and the many small resin and white-metal castings are packaged in ziplock bags. The photoetched sheet is usually inside a protective clear sleeve located at the bottom of the box. The instructions usually list all the parts, and the first thing you should do is take an inventory of everything to ensure that you have all the parts and that they are not damaged.

Most resin kit manufacturers are good about including all the parts necessary to build the kit, but occasionally some are missing. Contact the manufacturer as soon as possible to have lost or damaged parts replaced. Review the instructions carefully and become familiar with the parts and the suggested assembly sequences. Resin kits, like their plastic counterparts, can be built using just about any assembly sequence, and the one you choose will depend on whether you are building a full-hull display or a waterline display, as well as other factors, including color scheme and scale. The plastic bin organizers I mentioned in Chapter 1 are a must when you are building resin kits, because all the parts are bagged, and the best way to take inventory, organize, and separate them is to use the bin organizers.

Working with resin is easy as long as you follow a few simple guidelines. First, be very careful when removing resin pour plugs from parts. Resin is easy to cut and sand, so be careful not to overdo it. I recommend cutting the plugs down to as

The first step in assembling a resin ship hull is to remove the pour plug if there is one. The easiest way to do this is with a disk sander. Be careful that you don't oversand, and check your work frequently.

small an area as possible using a razor saw, then sanding smooth. Do this by running the part across a stationary piece of sandpaper in a figure-eight motion. Rotate the part so you don't sand off too much resin on one side. Take your time and check your work frequently.

Once you get the excess off, scrub the parts with a soft toothbrush and mild soap in warm water to remove mold release agents and resin dust. Wear a dust mask when sanding resin, as the dust particles should not be inhaled. One way to reduce such dust is to wet-sand. When wet-sanding, use waterproof sandpaper—the brands typically in hobby stores are Testors and K&S Engineering sandpaper. Both are waterproof. Another great source for waterproof sandpaper is automotive stores.

I usually use thumbtacks to hold the sandpaper stationary and flat, and I have a special length of pine, which is perfectly flat, that I pin the sandpaper to. I then dip the part into water and begin sanding, frequently dipping to remove the resin slug and to add more water to the process. Another benefit to wet-sanding is that it keeps the sandpaper from becoming clogged with resin, so it will last longer.

While the quality of resin castings for ship models is very good, you still get an occasional void or air bubble to be filled. Some modelers may complain about these occasional problems, but I look at it this way: injection-molded models have seams to repair, mold seam lines to scrape off, and indentations to fill, and resin parts have pour plugs and occasional voids and air bubbles. It's six of one or half a dozen of the other. Personally, I like resin superstructure parts because you only need to remove their pour plugs—no gluing halves together, no removing of seams, and no loss of detail. The only thing you have to be careful of is ensuring that the surfaces from which you removed the plugs are flat and straight. Then, when you position them, they won't be slanted or skewed to one side.

Voids or air bubbles are easy to fill with super glue, putty, Evergreen strip stock, or resin. For voids on flat or large curved surfaces, use thick-gel super glue or resin. Testors putty also works well. For small air bubbles, use a thin super glue applied with a small-diameter wire applicator, or else use automotive crack filler. Sometimes the air bubbles are so small that the surface tension of the super glue will not allow it to seep into the tiny area. In these cases use automotive crack filler or, if you are using super glue, enlarge the hole slightly with a drill bit. I have found myself using automotive crack filler more and more these days to deal with small voids because it's easy to use, dries fast, wet-sands easily, and blends in perfectly.

Super glue accelerator will not affect resin, so you can use it to speed up the drying of super glue. You can also use Evergreen strip stock to fix small shapes and take care of problems in corners, on edges, or on the rims of circular shapes. Use a strip size that fits into the hole, dip the tip of the plastic in a puddle of super glue, and insert the tip of the strip into the hole. When the glue is dry, cut the plastic and trim and sand to shape.

Parts may also be warped or bent. You can sometimes correct them by submerging them in hot tap water and then straightening them out. You must secure the part in its new position until it cools; otherwise, it may snap back to its former shape as resin sometimes does. You can also use a hair dryer, but be careful not to melt or distort the part. If you don't feel comfortable trying to fix the problem, return the kit—most resin manufacturers will gladly replace a kit or defective part.

Once you have fixed any problems, clean the parts again to remove dirt and resin dust. Give them a final cleaning with Polly-S paint preparation cleaner and then apply a coat of primer. The primer will act as a final check for any voids or bubbles you may have missed. They are easy to miss, especially with light-colored resin parts. Your eyes will have a tendency to become "snow blind" when looking at them because of their uniform light color. Now you are ready for final painting and assembly.

Resin sometimes shrinks. While this is usually not a problem on small parts such as superstructure shapes and smaller fittings, on large pieces like hulls it can be a real problem. Typically, resin hulls are split at the water line and you have to glue the upper and lower hulls together to get a

Some resin manufacturers like Classic Warships don't have resin pour plugs on their ship hulls, but you still have to flatten the gluing surface. The easiest way to do this on large models is with a hand sander.

full-hull kit. The shrinkage usually occurs along its length, but only slightly. The real problem is with the width. Sometimes the shrinkage can be as much as 1/8 inch. Trying to fix this after you have glued the hull halves is impossible, especially if the hull has a torpedo bulge.

Cutting up the lower hull into sections, butting up the edges, gluing them into place, and then filling the gaps with resin is by far the easiest and quickest way to fix this problem. Some manufacturers produce full-hull kits, which solves this shrinkage problem, but they are very difficult to cast. The deck detail is often marred by small surface voids.

White-metal parts are easy to work with, as they can be scraped, sanded, and shaped just like plastic. White metal, like resin, can have mold release agents on it, so give it a good cleaning with an enamel-based paint thinner. Sometimes the surfaces of white metal can have minute voids, which can easily be filled with super glue.

White-metal parts typically have very small seam lines, much like injection-molded parts, although they can be difficult to see. Scrape and sand the white-metal seam lines just as if they were plastic. When you are satisfied with your work, give the parts a coat of primer. The gray color will highlight anything you may have missed. To get the primer to blend in, sand the surface with 600-grit sandpaper, coat the bare area with primer, and then give the entire part a coat. White-metal parts are flexible and as a consequence masts and gun barrels are sometimes bent when you get them. To bend them back into shape, simply roll them gently across your workbench and carefully work out kinks with flat-faced needle-nose pliers.

The assembly sequence for building resin ship kits is pretty much the same as plastic kits. Start with the hull, paint it, mount it on the display base, and then start on the superstructure. Once these parts are cleaned up, painted, and installed, add photoetched details and railings, the fittings and guns, and finally the rigging.

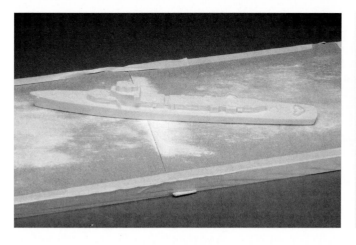

Another way to remove the plug or flatten the surface is to thumb-tack sandpaper to a flat surface and run the ship hull across it.

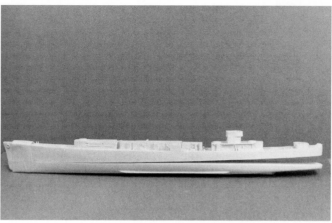

Sometimes resin hulls are warped slightly upward, but this is an easy problem to fix.

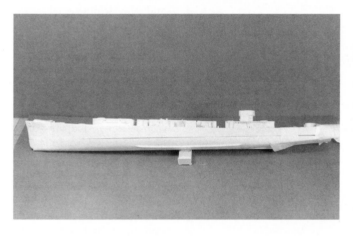

To fix these types of warps, simply tape the hull together tightly with masking tape when gluing.

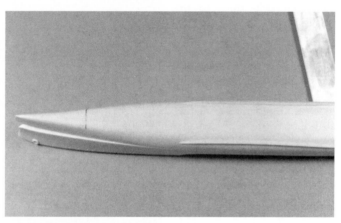

A hull warp along the center line, commonly known as a banana warp, usually occurs on the lower hull of smaller kits.

The first step in fixing this type of problem is to cut the lower hull, using a razor saw, where the warp starts.

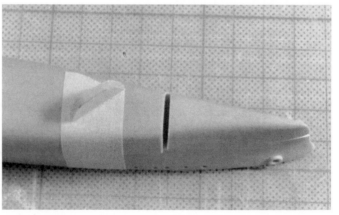

Next, glue the lower hull in place, butting the edges of the hull together. After the glue is dry, tape up the sides where the gap occurs, leaving the gap at the bottom of the hull so you can pour resin into it.

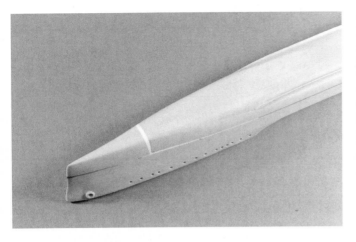

Here you can see that resin has filled the gap. It has also seeped into the small void between the upper and lower hull. Once the resin cures, sand and shape it.

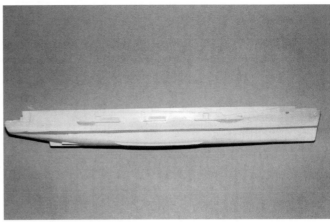

On ship hulls that fit together well, all you have to do once you remove the pour plugs is glue the hull halves together. Here, MB Models 1/350 scale *USS Gambier Bay* is getting its first coat of putty filler between the upper and lower hull. To limit the spread of putty, simply lay masking tape down on both sides of the pour line, apply the putty, then lift up the tape before the putty dries.

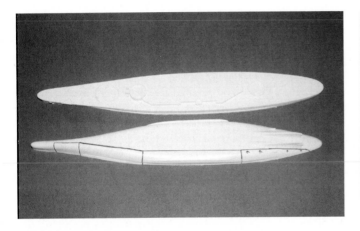

On large scale resin ship models you sometimes get shrinkage in the width of the lower hull. When this happens the only alternative is to cut the lower hull into sections. The first step in this process is to mark the cut lines.

The easiest way to cut large resin pieces is on a band saw, although it is possible to do with a hacksaw.

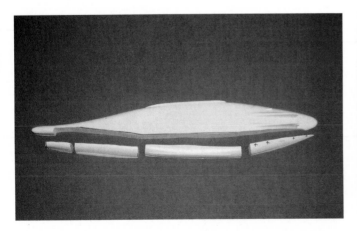

Cut up the lower hull parts; they are ready now ready to glue to the upper hull.

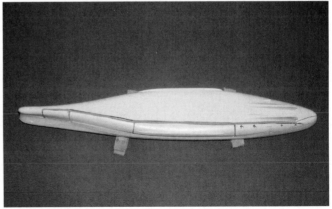

Glue the lower hull and upper hull parts together, and butt the individual parts against the outer face of the hulls. This results in large gaps that need to be filled.

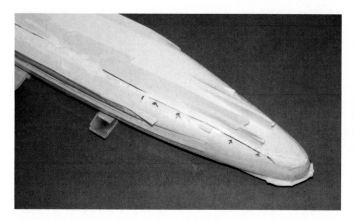

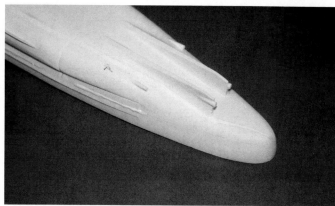

Use clear tape to seal the gaps on the sides of the hull, as well as the thin void line between the upper and lower hull. Then apply masking tape along the bottom of the hull along the gap line to prevent resin overflow from attaching itself to the hull. Then pour resin into the gaps in stages. The clear tape allows you to monitor the height of the resin as it fills the voids.

Remove the tape and then apply additional resin to the thin void lines between the upper and lower hull using a plastic syringe applicator like the ones Micro Mark sells. Initial sanding has begun to contour the resin into the hull and to reshape some areas. To reduce the amount of resin dust, simply wet-sand, or else fill your bathtub with water. Sand the hull in the tub using waterproof sandpaper.

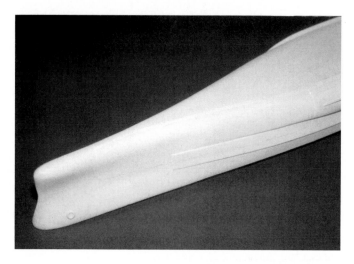

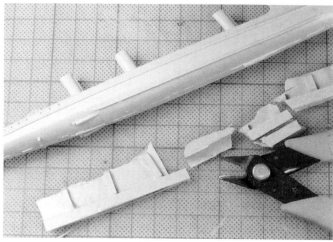

Sand the hull smooth, blending in the resin completely along the sides of the hull and filling in the voids. This approach of cutting up the hull and using resin as a filler is by far the easiest way to deal with the common problem of resin shrinkage.

For one-piece hulls simply cut off the pour line with a set of sprue cutters.

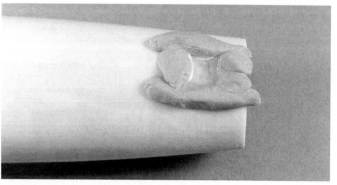

The next step is to scrape the bottom of the resin hull flat using a number 11 X-acto blade. Once this is complete, you can wet-sand the bottom of the hull smooth.

To fix small voids, you can use either putty or resin. Create a small box around a void using clay, and pour resin into the void.

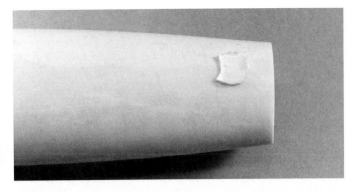

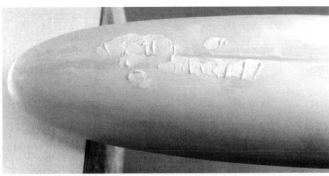

The next step is to remove the clay and then wet-sand the resin and blend it into the hull.

Use putty to fill small voids. Apply it to a piece of paper and use an X-acto blade to cut small amounts and apply them sparingly. Wet-sand the putty and blend it into the hull. To thin it out, mix a small amount with a drop or two of alcohol.

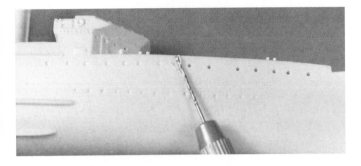

You'll have to drill out portholes on resin ship models to make them more realistic.

After you prime the hull it's a good idea to check it one more time for pinholes and voids that you may have missed. Simply fill these voids with automotive scratch filler, wet-sand them smooth, and then reprime.

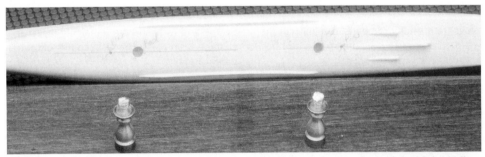

To display resin ship models on brass pedestals, strike a center line on the bottom of the hull and then drill holes in their proper locations. Thick-gel super glue or two-part epoxy works well to attach pedestals to the resin.

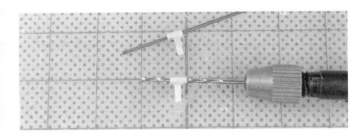

Drill out resin or white metal V struts in the same way as their plastic counterparts. Use several sizes of drill bits, working up to the size you need.

Bend photoetched propellers slightly to simulate the curve of real propellers.

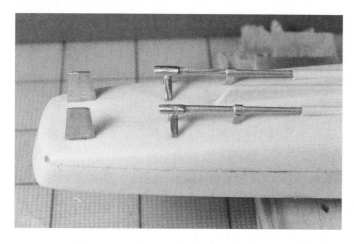

Some kits have one-piece white-metal shaft and V strut castings. Be careful when bending these parts back into shape, and be sure they look alike.

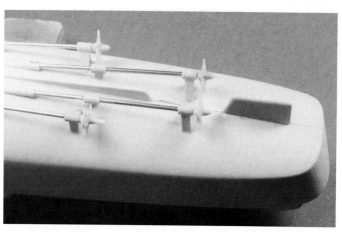

The shafts, struts, rudder, and props have been installed on this 1/350 scale Classic Warships *Cleveland*-class cruiser kit. Don't glue the shafts, which are brass, or the propellers into place until after you paint the hull.

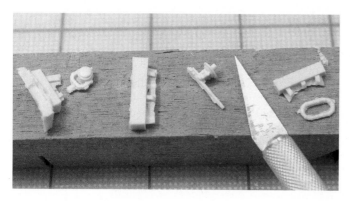

To remove the pour plugs from small resin parts, carefully cut the parts from the plugs on a hard surface using the tip of a number 11 X-acto blade.

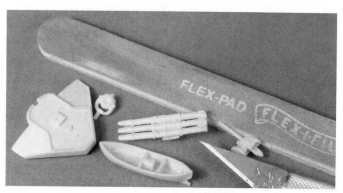

Scrape and wet-sand the remaining resin. Be very careful when sanding resin parts. The resin comes off quickly, so check your work carefully.

You can remove the pour plugs quickly from large resin superstructure parts by using a sanding disk. Here again, check your work frequently. I like to get most of the resin off and then finish it by running the part across a stationary piece of sandpaper.

Small resin parts can have thick pour plugs, but here again be careful. Wet-sanding can remove the plug and eliminate any resin dust.

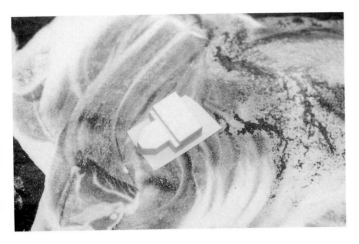

Some manufacturers like Classic Warships have thin pour plugs that overlap the part. This can be an advantage because as the resin gets thinner you can clearly see your progress. Use a figure-eight motion to sand resin and rotate the part frequently.

You can remove some pour plugs with a razor saw and then sand them smooth.

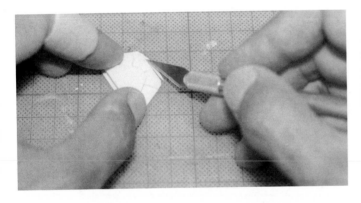

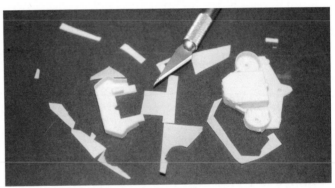

Sometimes pour plugs are very thin. Remove them with a number 11 X-acto blade. Be sure to angle the blade slightly towards the part to minimize the amount of scraping and sanding you will have to do.

Removing the pour plugs on parts can be a messy process even if you are just cutting off the resin.

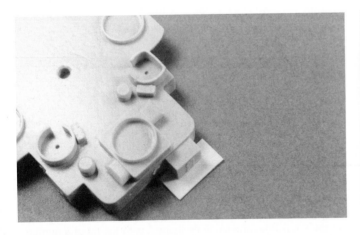

Sometimes you can oversand an outer area, but the fix is simple. Glue a small section of sheet stock to the base of the part and blend it in. Be sure that the entire surface of the sheet has a very thin coat of glue on it. When the glue is dry, trim the excess and sand around the base of the part to blend in the plastic.

Sometimes you can oversand the entire surface of the part. In these cases, simply glue a plastic sheet to the base of the part, trim the edges, and then sand it to the correct thickness.

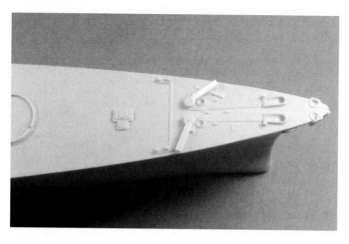

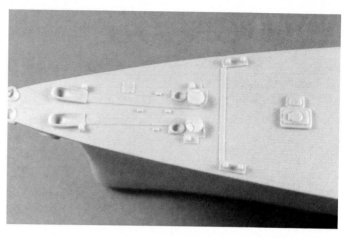

Fixing deck surface flaws can be very challenging with resin ship models, but like almost everything the solutions are usually easy. Glue small lengths of Evergreen strip stock into place. Slightly reshape the voids to accept the square ends of the stock, and apply super glue to the entire surface to provide a good coating.

Cut the lengths of plastic, and shape and contour the parts with a small length of a Flex-I-File sanding stick.

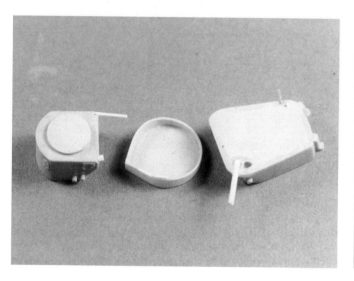

Voids can also occur along edges. Here again, glue small lengths of various thickness of Evergreen strip stock into the voids.

Clean up the parts and sand the strip stock into shape. After you paint the parts, you will not be able to tell where the voids were.

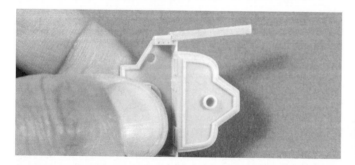

This void is of particular interest because it is located in an area where it is easy to damage surrounding detail. Glue a large over-sized length of scrap resin into place after reshaping the void to accept the filler piece.

Cut the scrap resin and carefully shape it with the tip of a number 11 X-acto blade. Then sand it smooth without damaging any of the surrounding detail.

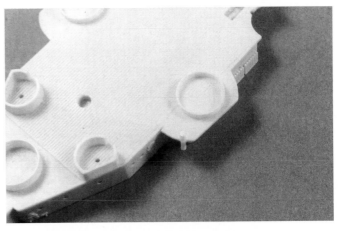

These photos show how to fix deck voids using scrap lengths of Evergreen strip stock. The concern here is that you will oversand the deck and make the problem worse. The trick is to use a thickness of plastic just slightly larger than the resin, or if it is on the edge, use a rod shape.

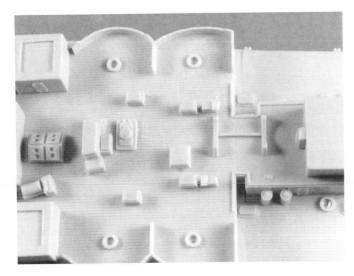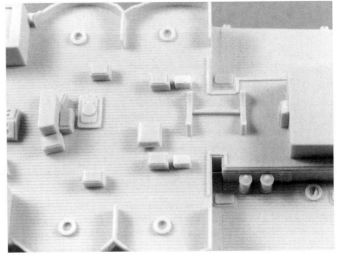

The gun boxes on this kit were not fully formed. Cut very small pieces of plastic almost to the exact shape of the gun boxes and glue them into place.

After the glue dries, scrape the sides of the plastic with the tip of a number 11 X-acto blade until they blend into the gun box shape and sand the tops carefully.

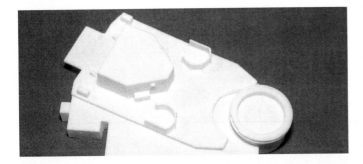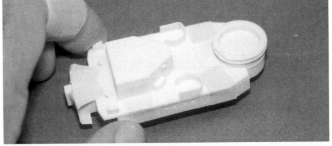

Most resin superstructure parts are one-piece castings, but occasionally some are two-piece castings. Carefully trim the upper part and check the fit.

Apply thick-gel super glue or two-part epoxy to the under surface, position the part, and use strips of masking tape to secure it. The glue or epoxy will give you some time to position the part. In this case, the upper part was slightly wider than the lower, so the surface detail on the sides of the superstructure will have to be replaced.

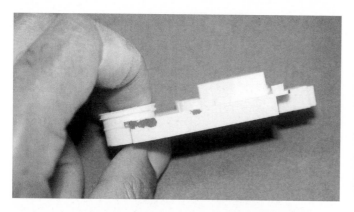

Smooth the sides by running them across a stationary piece of sandpaper. Then fill the remaining voids with automotive scratch filler.

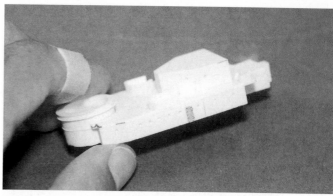

Replace the hatches with Gold Medal Models photoetched hatches, redrill the portholes, and replace the flat sides of the splinter shields with Evergreen strip stock.

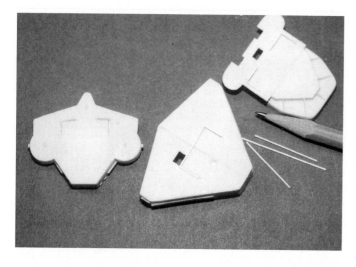

When stacking resin superstructure parts, make positioning lips or tabs of some sort to help you position the parts when you are ready to glue them into place. Carefully position one level on top of another, mark around the edges with a sharp pencil, and then glue thin strips of Evergreen strip to the underside, creating a positioning lip.

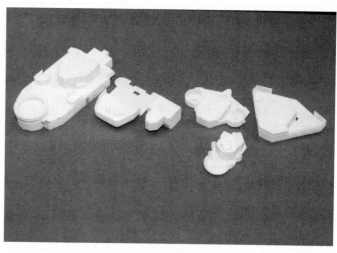

Here is the complete forward superstructure for Classic Warships 1/350 scale *USS Quincy* ready to be painted. All the parts have been cleaned up and positioning lips have been added to the undersides of the parts.

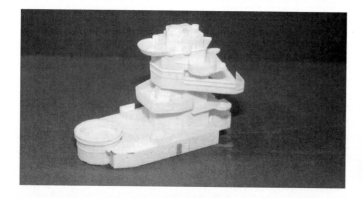

Stack the parts for a final check before priming. Be sure that the parts are not leaning to the side or skewed.

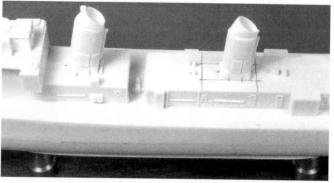

Another way to position parts is to use small lengths of brass rod. First position the part and then mark locations on the base of the part and on the deck. Then remove the part and connect the marked locations with lines. The connecting points between the lines are where to drill the holes for the brass rod.

Draw the lines, drill the holes, and glue the brass rod lengths into place.

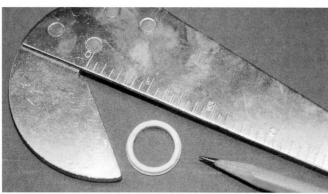

A really handy tool to have is a center locator for disks. This simple tool locates not only the center of a disk for drilling, but also the line through the center, which is great when you have to glue a turret base to the deck.

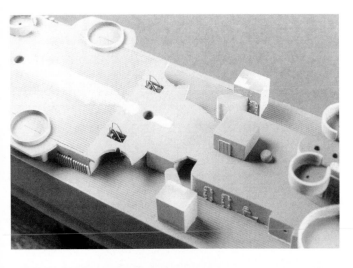

Building up resin superstructures works the same way as building plastic ones. Start at the base and work upward, adding detail as you go. Glue the base level of Classic Warships *USS Miami* in place, add the inclined ladders, and scrape the paint in preparation for gluing the next layer.

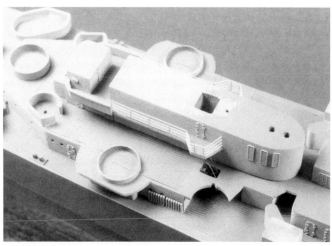

The next layer is now in place. Add the wing railings.

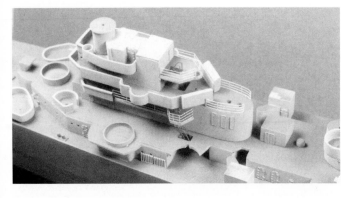

This superstructure is really taking shape. Add more levels, inclined ladders, and railings. Paint all the levels before installing them.

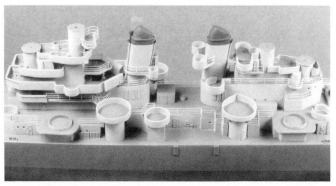

Add the rear superstructure and stacks, along with more railings.

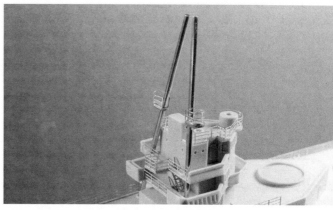

Next add the masts and rigging. Classic Warships *Cleveland*-class cruiser of the *USS Miami* is typical of a good resin kit in that the parts are well engineered and well cast. The same can be said of MB Models and White Ensign Models kits.

Building towers with brass rod can be a bit tricky because it can be difficult to ensure that the tower is sitting straight and level. I like to work with the legs first, get them set into place, and add detail as I work my way up.

Here the forward tower on MB Models 1/350 scale *USS Houston* is complete and ready for painting.

Classic Warships *USS Ward* has a hollow bridge deck with some photoetched details. You can also add some additional details if you are a real detail person. Be sure to paint the interior before you glue the bridge roof on.

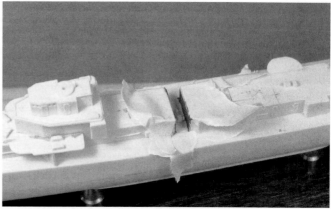

The tricky part is adding the photoetched window frame. Be very careful when bending the frame around the superstructure. To fair it into place, run a very small bead of super glue around the lower and upper connection points and carefully sand it down.

Another example of using photoetched parts is on MB Models *Gearing*-class destroyer. Here again paint the interior before you add the photoetching.

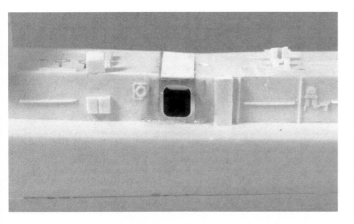

After bending the photoetching into shape and gluing it into place, blend it into the side of the superstructure.

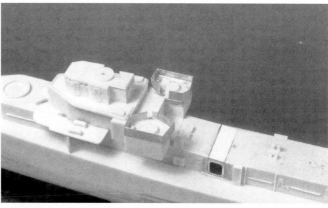

When gluing photoetched parts, especially gun shields, be sure to sand the base of the photoetching so that the glue will adhere to the metal.

Sometimes photoetched parts do not fit correctly. In this case just use Evergreen strip stock. Start at the front and then work your way around the base, gluing as you go.

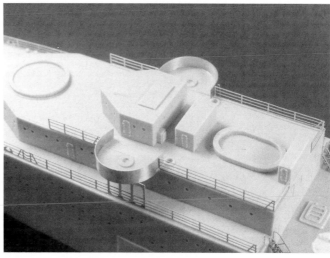

Sometimes combinations of resin parts and photoetching can make up a part. Here the forward 5/25 gun location bases of MB Models USS Houston are made of resin, and the shields are made from photoetching.

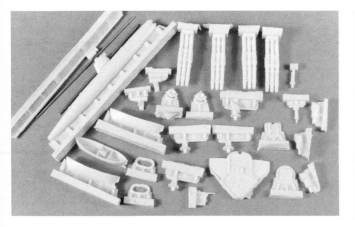

Resin ship kits can have a lot of parts, so I recommend that you purchase plastic bin organizers, which can be found in arts and crafts stores.

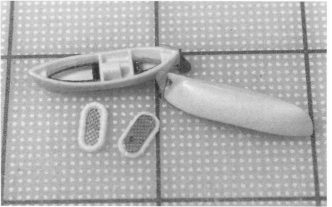

Adding small photoetched detail parts to resin casting can be very time-consuming. Just go slow, and when you get nervous, set the kit aside.

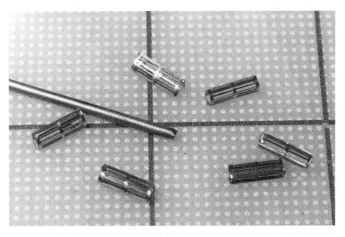

These small photoetched net holders were shaped with a Waldron punch tool, which just happened to be the right diameter.

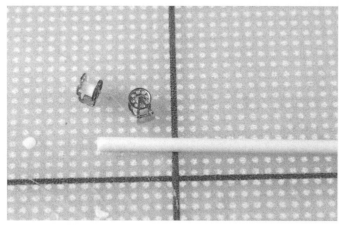

These photoetched hose reels needed center sections, made from small lengths of rod.

These gun director towers are a combination of white metal and photoetched parts. When folding box shapes, be careful not to distort the shape of the box.

Add detail to these torpedo cranes with small lengths of brass rod, glued into place with super glue.

Wood dowels of all diameters are very handy when shaping photoetched parts, so be sure to have a good supply on hand.

I like to check the fit of all the small parts before assembling superstructure parts. Then I don't find out after it's too late that the holes should be larger or deeper.

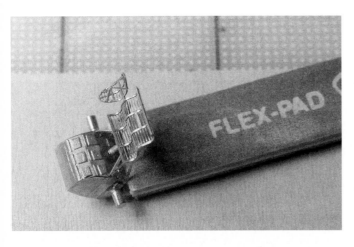

This MB Models Mk-37 radar is now ready to be painted. There is a lot of detail packed into resin kits if you just take the time to assemble them and work out the minor kinks.

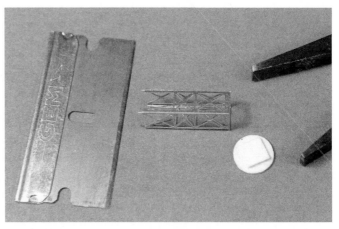

Single-edge razor blades are very handy. They can assist you when you're bending photoetched parts.

Always check the fit of photoetched towers into their deck locations. Chances are at least one of the locating holes is slightly off.

The photoetched details for biplanes are very small. I suggest that you take your time with these small parts. I like to position and glue the parts on the lower wing and fuselage, paint the aircraft, and then glue the upper wing in place.

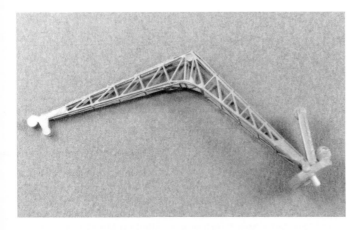

This Classic Warships photoetched crane is made up of a cast resin base and back arm and a photoetched frame. After you add the cable, this crane will be ready to install onto the deck.

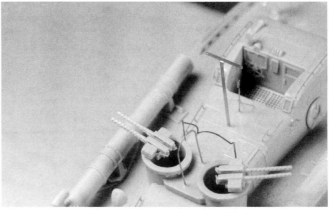

Photoetched details can be very delicate, but if you take your time they can add a high level of detail to your model. Classic Warships 77-foot Elco PT boat has several delicate photoetched parts, but they are easy to work with.

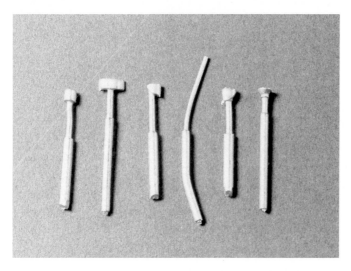

White-metal parts are sometimes bent, but they can easily be straightened out using a set of flat-nose pliers or by just rolling them on a flat surface.

Here are the same white-metal parts installed on Toms Modelworks 1/192 scale SSBN *Ethan Allen*-class sub.

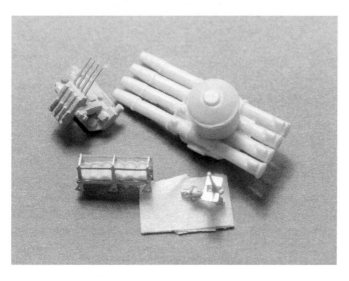

Resin kits typically use combinations of resin and white metal along with photoetching to make up torpedo, depth charge, and small caliber guns.

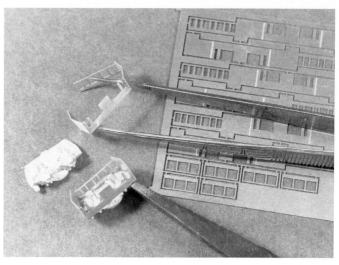

The photoetched gun shields on MB Models 40mm gun bases can be very tricky. Be sure you make them all look the same.

Drill out white-metal guns just like plastic.

Here is the same twin 5-inch gun installed on MB Models 1/350 scale *USS Gearing*. The drilled-out guns really add a greater level of detail.

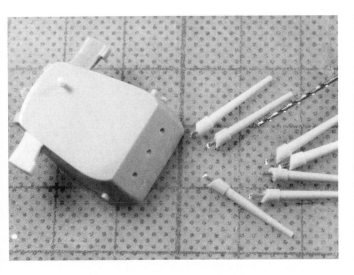

I like to use small lengths of brass rod to both position and strengthen large gun barrels.

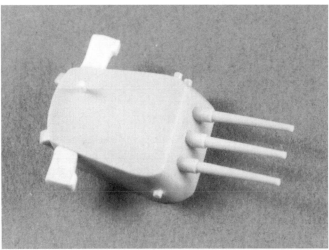

The barrels are installed and the turret is ready for its white glue application around the bases of the barrels to simulate blast bags.

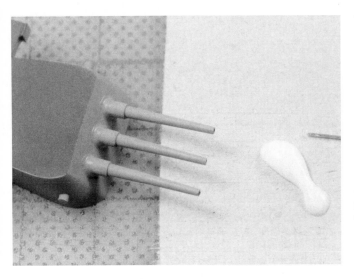

Apply the white glue carefully with a thin length of brass rod around the entire circumference of the barrel. The trick here is to get all three to look almost the same.

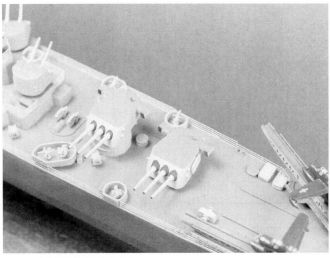

The guns and blast bags have been painted and installed on Classic Warships 1/350 scale *USS Miami*.

Almost all resin kits come with white-metal masts. If you plan to add rigging, I recommend that you replace the mast with brass rod, because white metal has a tendency to bend. You can install the brass length as is or you can slightly contour it using a Dremel drill press and vise to make a simple lathe.

Use a file and a Flex-I-File sanding stick to grind off some of the brass and smooth it out.

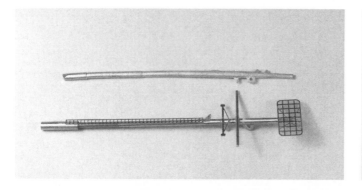

Here is the white-metal mast and the new brass rod mast with kit details added.

Here the same mast is being form-fitted into place on MB Models 1/350 scale *USS Gearing.*

This 1/350 scale *USS Ward* kit has a resin forward mast with photoetched yardarm. Although it did not bend when I rigged the kit, I had to be very careful not to skew the entire mast.

Set up the rear mast on the same model with a thin-diameter length of brass wire and a photoetched yardarm. With small-diameter wire there is no need to contour its length.

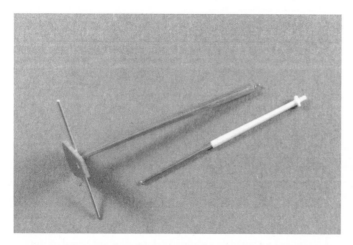

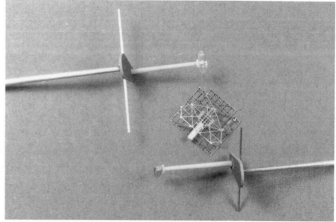

Build up masts in stages or subassemblies. I like to add lengths of brass wire to the bases of masts to strengthen them. Cut the brass rod protruding from the base of the smaller resin mast to length, and then glue it to the mast platform.

These masts are for Classic Warships 1/350 scale *USS Miami.* The radar will be added after the masts are painted, installed, and rigged.

Photo Gallery

The Fleet

HMS King George V detailed with Gold Medal Models photoetched set.
Manufactured by Tamiya, Inc. 1/350 scale kit built by Scott Weller

ABOVE: *Cleveland*-class cruiser *USS Miami.* Resin kit manufactured by Classic Warships. 1/350 scale kit built by Mike Ashey

OPPOSITE: *USS Yorktown* (1/350 scale kit manufactured by Tom's Modelworks) accompanied by *Fletcher*-class destroyer (1/350 scale kit manufactured by Tamiya), detailed with Gold Medal Models and Tom's Modelworks photoetching. Models built by Kelly Quirk

ABOVE: 77-Foot Eleco Pt 31 boat as she appeared in late December 1941. Resin kit manufactured by Classic Warships. 1/96 scale kit built by Mike Ashey

RIGHT: World War II and postwar U.S. submarines: *Gato*-class early and late World War II subs. *Balao*-class postwar subs with different sails. Resin kits manufactured by Tom's Modelworks. 1/350 scale kits built by Bill Teehan

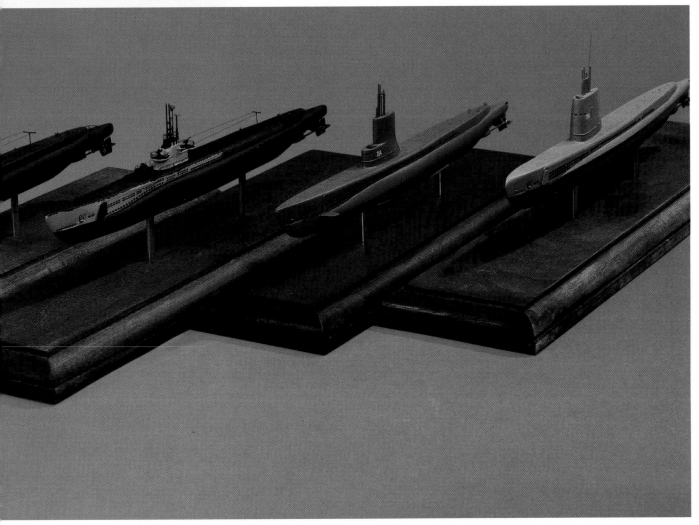

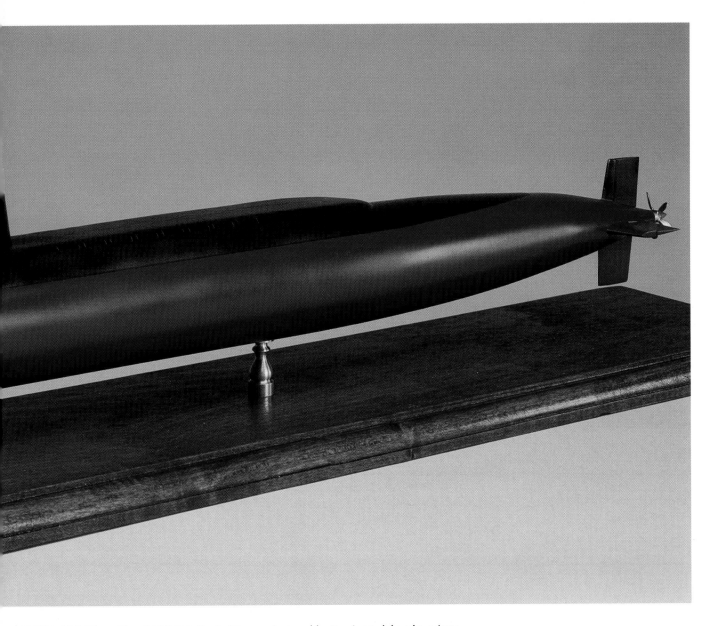

ABOVE: *USS Ethan Allen* SSBN 608. Resin kit manufactured by Tom's Modelworks. 1/192
scale kit built by Mike Ashey

LEFT: *USS Peterson* detailed with Gold Medal Models photoetched sets. Manufactured by
DML, Inc. 1/350 scale kit built by Mike Ashey

USS Missouri detailed with Gold Medal Models photoetched set.
Manufactured by Tamiya, Inc. 1/350 scale kit built by Mike Ashey

February 23, 1942 at 7:07 pm the California coast at Elwood resolved the First Naval Bombardment of the U.S. mainland by a Foreign power since the War of 1812. Japanese Imperial Navy Submarine I-17, commanded by Kozo Nishino, fired [25] 5.5" shells over a 40 minute period at coastal oil tank farm installations (Bell Oil Company). This was less than three months after the Pearl Harbor attack. Fear gripped west coast cities and the Navy / Coast Guard, short of everything including coastal patrol craft, pressed into service trawlers such as the "Carol" (Hull # 37) for coastal picket duty. Armament typically consisted of a 3" 50 Bow Gun and a 20 mm single M4 mount. Model (1/96 scale) depicts the "Carol" in civilian Paint in drydock at time of refit (March 1942). Model, base, case, by Richard Boutin, Sr. Completed Fall of 1997.

U-BOOT TYP 206A

U-BOAT TYPE 206A

TWENTY SIX YEARS AFTER WORLD WAR II, THIS U-BOAT AT 500 TONS WAS SMALL REPRESENTING A NEW BREED OF DIESEL / ELECTRIC SUBMARINES OF OPTIMUM MANEUVERABILITY, LOW SOUND RADIATION AND (8) BOW TUBES ACCOMMODATING WIRE GUIDED TORPEDOS CAPABLE OF GREAT ACCURACY AT EXTREME RANGE. HAS A (21) MAN CREW, SURFACE SPEED (17) KNOTS, SUBMERGED SPEED (12) KNOTS, WITH HANDLING CHARACTERISTICS SIMILAR TO SUBSEQUENT NUCLEAR AGE SUBMARINES. SCALE 1:144 MODEL, BASE, CASE BY RICHARD BOUTIN, AUGUST 1998.

ABOVE: Type 206A U-Boat (1970s-era submarine). Kit manufactured by Revell of Germany. 1/144 scale kit built by Richard Boutin, Sr.

UPPER LEFT: Armed North Atlantic fishing trawler (early 1942) with H&R Products guns. Manufactured by Lindberg, Inc. 1/90 scale kit built by Richard Boutin, Sr.

LEFT: "S" Boat Submarine. Resin Kit Manufactured by MB Models. 1/350 scale kit built by Lonnie Ottzen

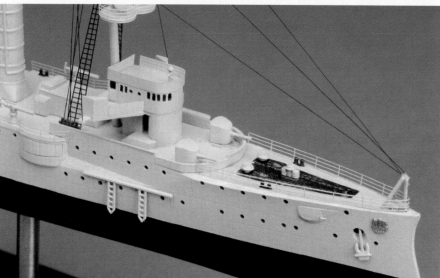

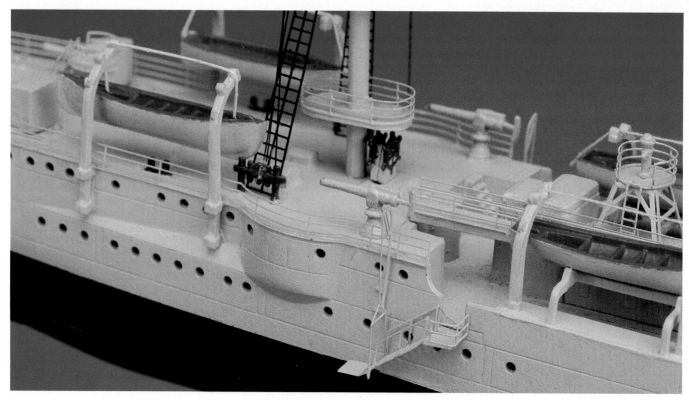

ABOVE: *HMS Belfast* with Gold Medal Models and White Ensign Models photo-etched sets. Manufactured by Airfix, Inc. 1/600 scale kit built by Bill Teehan

LEFT: *SMS Emden* with Gold Medal Models photoetched set. Kit manufactured by Revell, Inc. 1/350 scale kit built by Scott Weller

LEFT: *USS Sims* resin kit manufactured by Classic Warships. 1/192 scale kit built by Randy Chisum

BELOW: Scratchbuilt post-World War II gasoline tanker *USS Namakagon.* 1/192 scale model by Al Ross

Pt 109. 1/72 Scale Revell-Monogram kit with 37mm cannon from the
Hasegawa Jeep kit. Built By Phil Kirchmeier. Photo by Jim Forbes

Chapter Three

Scratchbuild & Detail Superstructure Shapes

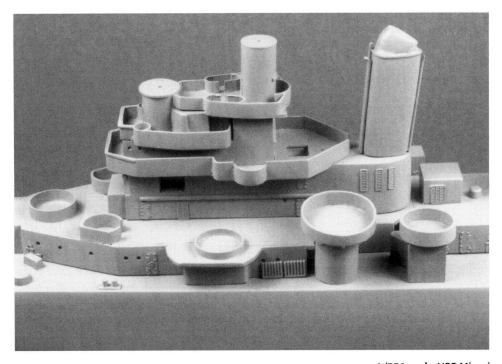

1/350 scale *USS Miami*

I n my first shipbuilding book (*Building and Detailing Scale Model Ships*, Kalmbach Publishing Co.), I showed you how to scratchbuild masts and guns, add gun and splinter shields, and modify kit superstructures. The next step in scratchbuilding is fabricating superstructure shapes from plastic sheet and then detailing them. To build up superstructure shapes with edges that are straight and true, or to incorporate angles, you'll need a very important piece of equipment—a variable-speed disk sander with an adjustable working surface. If you use a normal disk sander, you will melt the plastic as you try to shape it because the disk turns at such a high speed. Both Micro Mark Inc. and Model Expo Inc. sell variable-speed disk sanders ranging in sizes from 3 to 10 inches. They also sell sanders that are not variable speed but have attachments that provide variable-speed voltage to the sander.

You will need to work from reference materials such as drawings and pictures. The Floating Drydock has an excellent selection of drawings to choose from, and they also have a great library of black-and-white pictures of ships, including close-ups of superstructures. Another source of reference material is illustrated books on a particular ship. The Naval Institute Press has published several books on various classes of ships with side- and top-view drawings; with these books and a set of pictures, you can build pretty much whatever you want.

The subject I'll use as an example here is the super-structure of the cruiser *USS Brooklyn* CL-40 as she appeared in 1938 when launched. There are no drawings of this ship for this time period except the top- and side-view drawings done by Alan Raven and Arthur D. Baker III for the Naval Institute Press book *U.S. Cruisers,* by Norman Friedman. While the drawings in the book are small, if you know the actual length of the ship and measure the length of the drawings, you can easily calculate the approximate scale of the drawing.

There are several ways to determine size and scale. I calculated what the hull length should be in 1/350 scale and then used the length of the drawing to determine the percentage the drawing would need to be enlarged by to make it 1/350 scale, which was 278 percent. The one drawback to this process is that the lines on the blown-up drawings tend to become slightly distorted. I used the enlarged drawings as a basis to create another set of simple top- and side-view superstructure shape drawings.

These blown-up drawings will not always tell you everything about the shape of a particular superstructure level; that is why pictures are also important. I studied the pictures and carefully created the drawings. It took three tries until I was finally satisfied with the general appearance, size, proportion, and shape of the superstructure parts. If you are just starting out, do not try to create a set of

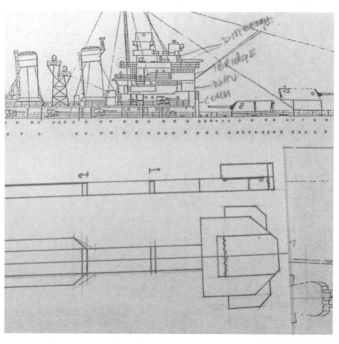

The first step in scratchbuilding superstructure parts is to acquire a set of drawings to work from. I enlarged these drawings for the *USS Brooklyn* by 278 percent and then drew a working set of drawings using photographs as a guide.

drawings on your own; instead, order a good set from the Floating Drydock, copy them so you don't ruin the originals, and then cut out the drawings of what you want to scratchbuild.

Superstructure shapes are usually a combination of squares and rectangles, and that is exactly what you need to make. Break down each part into subparts so you can easily make the different shapes and then just glue them together. The trick here is start from the same block of plastic so the shapes will all be exactly the same height, because there can be a slight difference in thickness of plastic sheets of a thousandth (.001) of an inch or so. Cut out a set of sheets larger than the superstructure part, glue them together, and square the block on the disk sander. Squaring the block is very important because if it isn't square your finished part won't look right. Next, cut the block into the subparts you need, cut out the top-view shapes from the drawings, glue them to the blocks with white glue, and sand them to shape. Then glue them together.

Once you get the first part glued, move on to the next part until you have completed all the superstructure parts. The next step is to add detail. I usually add the portholes first by marking the locations and then drilling them out. I then locate the hatches and fire hoses and use Gold Medal Models photoetched detail sheets to add these items. I use thick-gel super glue for adding photoetching as well as all other surface details. It gives me a few seconds of working time to ensure that the part is straight and level. Once you get the hang of it, you'll discover that scratchbuilding and detailing is easy and fun. You will also find that as you get better at it, you'll be making all kinds of neat stuff, including vents, storage boxes, gun boxes, and just about anything else you may need.

Decide how high the superstructure parts will be, and then pick plastic sheet sizes that when stacked will equal the height you want. Once you know the height and the shape, you are ready to glue the sheets together and go to work. Glue the plastic sheets together with thick-gel super glue. Smear the glue on each sheet so that it covers the entire surface. Then press the sheets firmly together, so the layers will be even and flat. Glue will pour out from between the layers of plastic, but that is to be expected. Once the glue has dried, add the next layer until the stack is complete.

It is important to get one vertical side perfectly flat and true. The easy way to do this is to set the stack against the miter and run one side against the disk sander until the face of the stack is perfectly flat. Then this first side becomes the working edge. Next, rotate the part so that the working edge sits firmly against the miter gauge and again feed the stack into the disk sander. When all four sides are finished, it should be perfect. Always check the base of the disk sander and the miter to ensure that they are set at 90 degrees.

Slowly work around the stack until all the edges are perfect and even. You are now ready to shape the superstructure, except for one last check.

I like to check my work, so I use a small machinist's square to double-check the sides.

To ensure that both the top and bottom surfaces are very smooth and that there are no scratches, run both surfaces across a piece of 400- to 600-grit sandpaper.

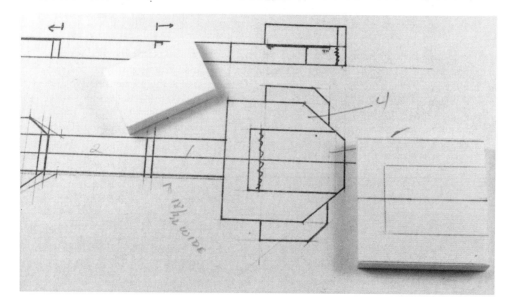

Next, start sizing the part to the drawings.

Use a razor saw to rough-cut the plastic; this will reduce the time it takes to sand the part to shape on the disk sander.

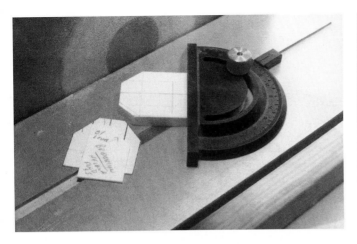

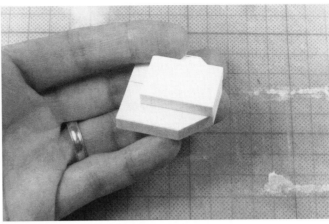

Set the miter to the angle you need with a gauge and then sand away. The gauge is simply the drawing glued to a plastic sheet that has been carefully cut to shape.

The first level is complete. Now set up the second level. Shape it on the disk sander, but since the edges of the second level are the same as the first, you can glue the piece into place before sanding.

Here you can see that the edges of both parts are perfect and the angles are the same. Once this part is painted it will be impossible to tell that it is made up of two separate pieces.

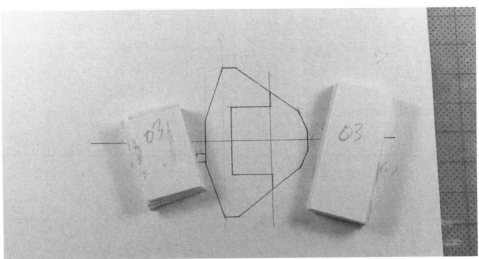

Break down complex shapes into small, simple shapes. This superstructure layer will be made up of a large base and two separate boxes, which you will glue together after shaping.

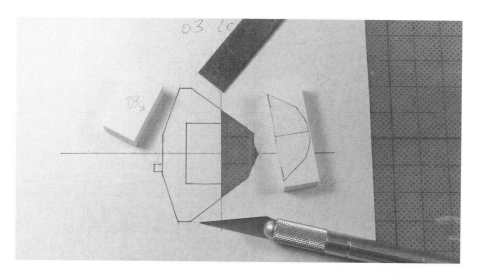

Cut out the pictures and then glue them to the blocks of plastic, being careful to ensure that the one edge of the drawing is perfectly aligned with one side of the block.

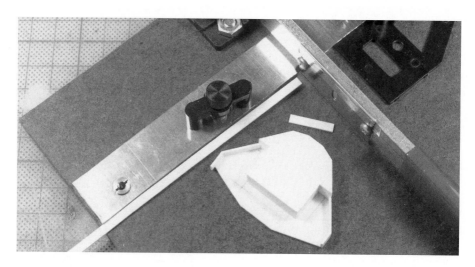

After completing the part, add splinter shields to the sides. Use a chopper to carefully cut the necessary lengths and angles. Here again, trial and error rules the day, so do not expect to get it right the first time.

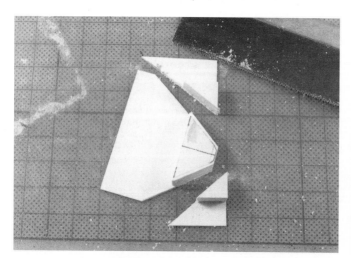

Use a razor saw to rough-cut the plastic before shaping it with the disk sander. Glue the block to the larger base prior to cutting, since both should be the same shape.

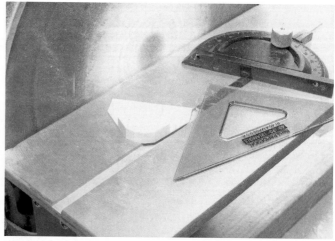

Shape the fine angles on the face of this superstructure part very carefully. It took two tries before I was satisfied with the shape of the part and the angles.

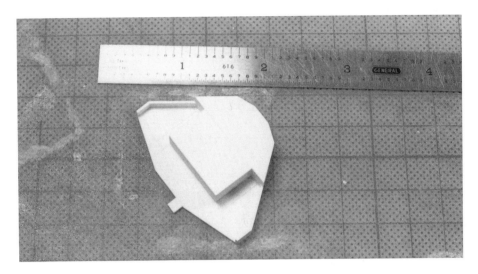

This superstructure part is now complete, except for the window framing that you will glue to the front face.

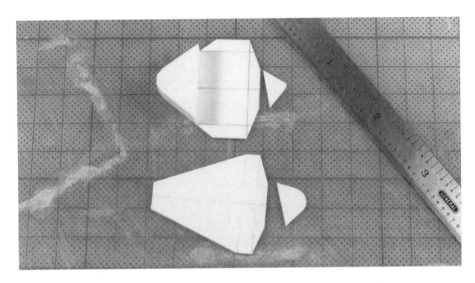

The trick of breaking down complex superstructure shapes into simpler ones also works for deck surfaces.

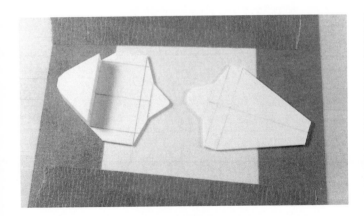

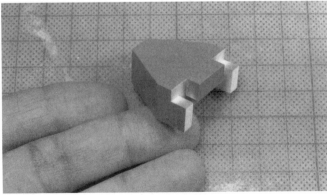

The easy way to glue these parts together is to run a tiny bead of super glue along the entire face of the gluing surface and mate the parts on top of a piece of wax paper. Super glue will not stick to wax. Once the glue is dry, carefully sand smooth. You'll have to replace the wax paper after a few gluing sessions.

Here is a superstructure part ready for detailing. Prime the surfaces to check for flaws.

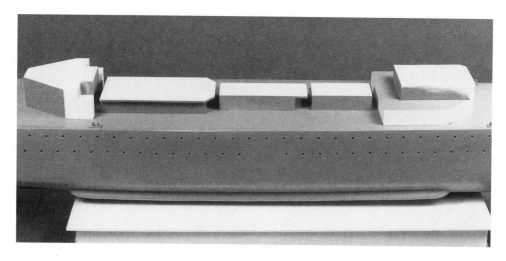

The main components of the superstructure of the *USS Brooklyn* in 1/350 scale are now beginning to take shape. I like to check and re-check parts once they are completed to ensure that they all fit together and that the general shapes of the parts work with one another.

The forward section of the superstructure is starting to look like something other than blocks of plastic. Add portholes, Gold Medal Models hatches, and other small details.

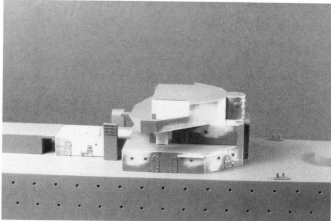

The third level of the superstructure is now complete.

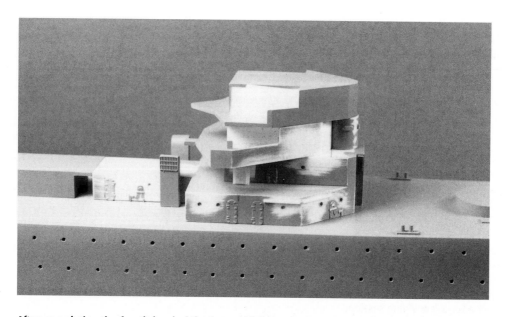

After completing the fourth level of the forward bridge superstructure, give it a fit check.

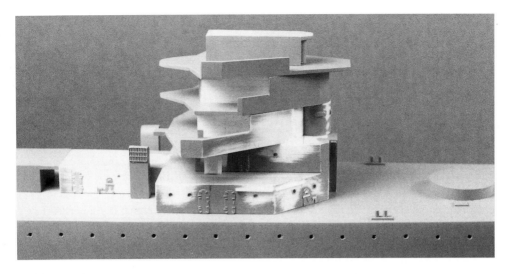

The last forward superstructure layer is now complete, and it has passed the fit check. Now it's time to do some detailing.

Make gun boxes using different sizes of Evergreen strip stock. The sheet that is lying flat is being used as a spacer for the gun box hatches. Use a chopper to cut the hatches.

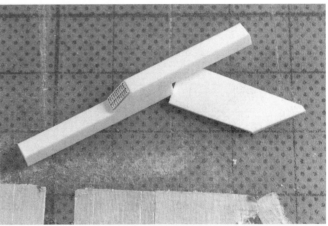

You can make vents of any shape and size using various sizes of plastic stock.

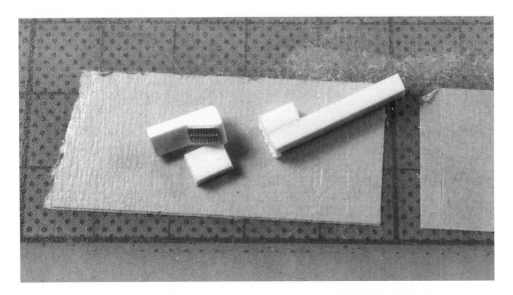

Cut the vent to size and shape it. I custom-made the small photoetched vent face from a sheet of photoetching.

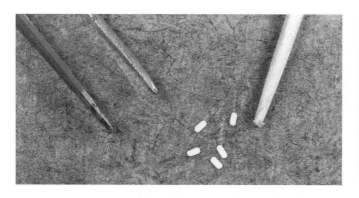

Small lengths of strip with the edges curved serve as lookout ports. Hold each length with tweezers while you touch the edges lightly with a sanding stick.

Glue the lookout ports to the superstructure surface. To help position these small parts, use a length of labeling tape.

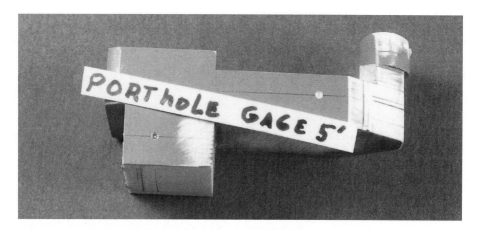

To ensure that all portholes are at the same height, make a gauge using a length of sheet stock. All you have to do is position the superstructure level on a flat surface and then run the gauge along the sides, using a pencil to draw the porthole line.

A small anvil that I made serves as a vertical gauge for setting hatches and other details. Here again, you need to set the superstructure part on a flat surface, set the gauge on the same surface, and then run a pencil along the vertical edges.

Add details to the side of the aft lower superstructure of the master pattern for a 1/350 scale *Cleveland*-class cruiser. The gas bottles came from Tamiya's *USS Missouri,* while the photoetched details are from Gold Medal Models.

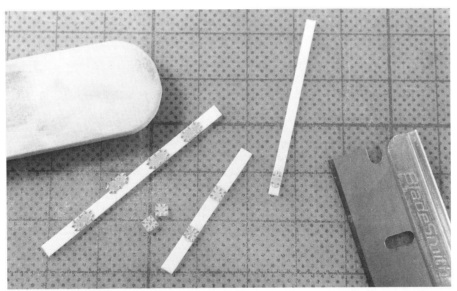

It's easy to make deck hatches by gluing photoetched hatches to small lengths of strip stock and then cutting them to shape.

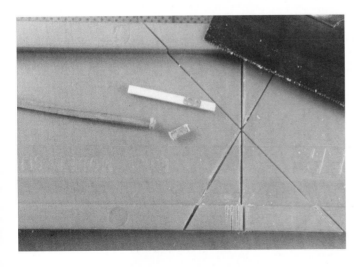

Make gun boxes in the same way, except that you'll have to cut them with a miter saw and then smooth the edges.

Shape the gun boxes, making them pretty much the same size. These gun boxes are ready for installation.

Apply the photoetched window framing and other details to the forward superstructure of the *USS Brooklyn*.

Add the photoetched window to the next superstructure layer; the assembly is now complete.

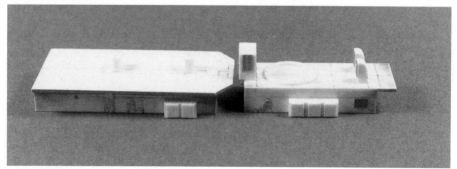

Add details to the center sections of the *USS Brooklyn's* superstructure. Note the storage and gun boxes made from plastic strip.

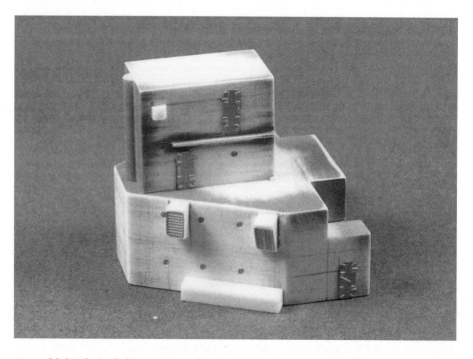

Now add details, including some small vents, to the aft superstructure.

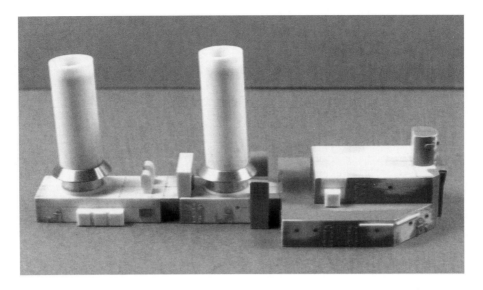

With the smokestacks complete, the center superstructure is now beginning to look like something other than blocks of plastic.

Here the forward superstructure of the *Brooklyn* is pretty much complete. Test-fit it onto the hull.

The aft superstructure is also now complete. It's sure neat to see a pile of plastic turned into superstructure parts, complete with portholes and hatches!

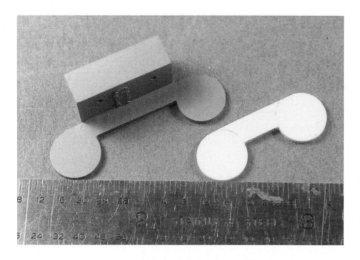

Make these shapes from a set of disks and a carefully cut-out center length of plastic. Use super glue as the filler.

These three parts will form the forward range finder tower for the *USS Brooklyn*.

Glue the parts together. After they're painted, they will become part of the forward superstructure.

To simulate frame supports, add small lengths of strip stock, cut to shape with a chopper, to the underside of this gun tub.

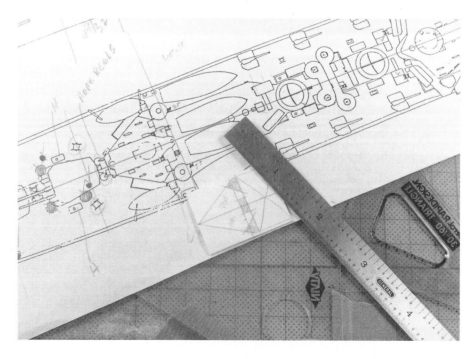

You can also make deck wings using the techniques demonstrated here. Start with a set of drawings and then transfer the drawings to sheet plastic.

Carefully cut out the rough shapes.

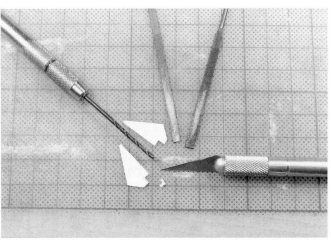

Then carefully fine-tune the shapes. Make sure that both shapes are exactly the same size.

Add splinter shields, cut to shape with a chopper. To help ensure that the shields are set at 90 degrees to the base, I use my machinist's square.

These bridge wing parts are now complete.

Chapter Four

Working with Brass and Stainless-Steel Photoetching

1/350 scale *USS West Virginia* built by Chris Preston

Photoetched sets are an absolute must for ship modeling, as they add a level of detail that can turn an average plastic model into a masterpiece. From multibar railings to inclined ladders, detailed radar sets to multilevel etched hatches and boat davits, these detail sets have it all! In addition, most resin ship kits have photoetched sheets that can include details ranging from railings to super-structure shapes.

Most photoetched sheets are made from brass, although a few small scale sets in 1/700 scale are done in stainless steel. Whether they are brass or stainless steel, they are made using the same technology that is used to make printed circuit boards. An image is imprinted onto a super thin sheet of brass or stainless steel and then the metal is immersed in a chemical that eats away the areas of the metal that are not imprinted with the image. The cost of photoetched sheets has been rising steadily over the past few years, mostly because of the cost of production and the expense of safely disposing of the chemical etching liquid. These detail sets are, however, still well worth the investment.

Always cut photoetching with a sharp blade and cut the parts on a hard surface such as glass or Plexiglas. Some manufacturers' instructions suggest that you can cut off parts with metal scissors. I recommend against this, since it is too easy to damage parts or cut into adjacent parts. Generally, it is easier to cut a photoetched part off its tree by leaving a little of the stub attached. You can easily remove the remaining stub from the part by using a number 11 X-acto blade and then smoothing the edge with a Flex-I-File sanding stick. Stainless-steel photoetched parts can be more difficult to cut off their trees because the metal is very strong, so be prepared to go through several blades.

As a general rule, photoetched sheets are between five thousandths (.005) and seven thousandths (.007) of an inch thick, but I have also worked with brass sheet as thin as three thousandths (.003) of an inch. With photoetched sheets getting thinner and thinner, you have to be extra careful not to distort the parts as you cut them off and clean them up. An important point here about cutting photoetching—wear your glasses or use a pair of safety glasses. Small photo-

etched parts, especially the stubs, have a bad habit of becoming projectiles when they are cut—so be careful and protect your eyes! I use Flex-I-File sanding sticks for a lot of cleanup work on photoetching. A great place to find sanding sticks is the nail care section of your local drug or grocery store. You will find a huge assortment in many colors and grits, and they are inexpensive.

Once a part is cut off, clean its surface by lightly running it across a stationary piece of 400- or 600-grit sandpaper taped to your workbench. Some modelers prefer to clean the surface of the entire detail sheet at once by laying the sheet flat and carefully running the sandpaper over it. This may be quicker, but you also stand a good chance of damaging individual parts. I recommend doing them one at a time. For long lengths of railings, lay the part on

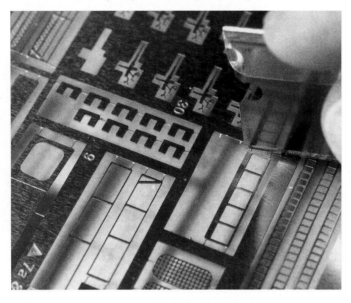

Always cut photoetching on a hard surface with a sharp blade. A piece of thick glass or a Plexiglas sheet works best. And be sure to wear safety glasses when cutting photoetching.

a flat surface and gently run the sandpaper across the surface of the part lengthwise and away from you. Do not slide the sandpaper back and forth. Only a few passes at the surface will clean it up—when it is shiny it is clean.

Cleaning up photoetched surfaces is a must if you're gluing sections together,

such as parts of an aircraft crane or a catapult launch, because the glue won't stick well to dirty photoetching. You'll have to clean the edges of railings and gun or splinter shields for the same reason; Flex-I-File sanding sticks are great for this. Gun and splinter shields that must be blended into the superstructure will need a strong bond with the resin. Sanding the surface will also rough it up, which helps the glue adhere better.

To get curves in photoetching, bend the part around a wood dowel or other round object with a diameter slightly smaller than you need—the photoetching will spring back a little. You can get sharp bends and angles with flat needle-nose pliers or by using two single-edge razor blades. If you are bending a part such as a crane into shape, take extra care to be sure that you're bending the entire length of the part at once. Then you'll get a straight bend. Make longer bends, such as on catapults, by using two single-edge razor blades. Hold the part down along the bending edge with one blade, and slide the other blade underneath along the bending edge. Then fold the part up.

Super glue is an excellent bonding agent for both brass and stainless-steel photoetching. When strength is not an issue, white glue also works well. Using white glue will allow you some flexibility in positioning pieces together, but be sure to prime the parts prior to gluing—the white glue will stick better to flat paint than to bare metal. White glue is also an excellent filler for cracks and voids when using photoetching. Be sure to prime photoetching before applying a paint finish.

To strengthen parts such as superstructure shapes and airplane catapults, use small lengths of Evergreen strip and round stock. Cut them to size and then glue them to the inside areas of these delicate parts.

To clean the surface of photoetching, carefully run the parts across a stationary piece of sandpaper. If the parts are delicate, do not run them back and forth, because this motion may damage them. A sweeping motion in one direction works best.

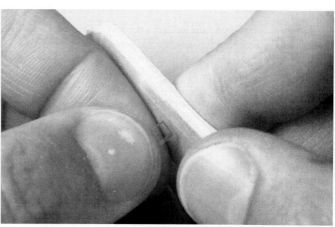

To clean the sides of photoetching, use a Flex-I-File sanding stick. It is especially important to clean the gluing surface of the railing to ensure that the super glue will stick.

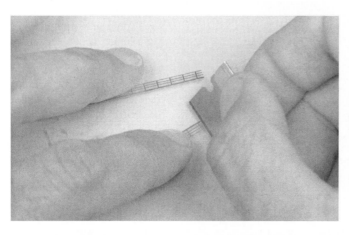

To trim the edges of railings, use a single-edge razor blade. Cut the entire length at one time so that the cut will be straight.

To get a sharp bend in photoetched railings, use a set of flat-faced needle-nose pliers to hold the part. Then bend the photoetching, using the edge of a single-edge razor blade.

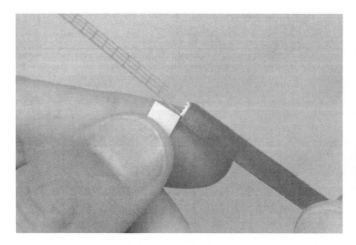

If you do not want to use a razor blade to make sharp bends, use a thick length of Evergreen strip.

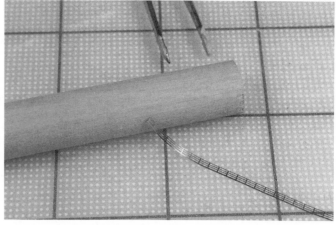

Curves in photoetched railings can be achieved with wood dowels or any other smooth-surface dowel or curved object. Since photoetching will spring back, use a dowel slightly smaller than the curve you need.

You can also make complete circles with wood dowels. Here again, it is best to use a slightly smaller dowel.

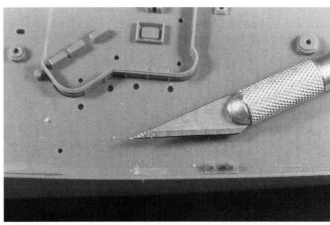

Planning the placement of photoetched railings is important. Plastic ship kits are not designed to accommodate them, so slight modifications are necessary. Here the locating outline for the bitts on Tamiya's 1/350 scale *USS Missouri* are scraped off so they will not interfere with the placement of the photoetching.

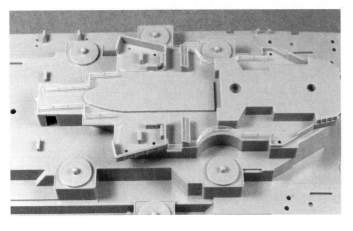

Whenever possible measure, cut, and form photoetching on the kit parts in the early stages of construction. Then if you have to add photoetching as you build up the superstructure, you can just glue the parts into place.

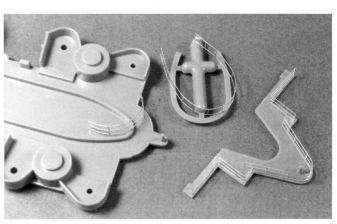

I like to form all the photoetched railings on small parts as well as on the large superstructure parts.

You can wrap long sections of railings around complex curves and bends, but you'll have to work carefully. Check your work often as you move around the part.

In almost all cases photoetched railings should be attached to the deck, but sometimes lengths of railings are designed to be glued to the sides of the part. If you glue the railings to the deck instead, the railings will interfere with other deck details.

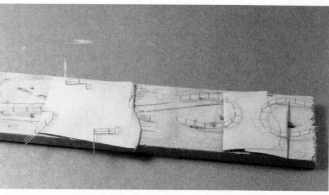

Whenever possible, work in subassemblies. Add the railings on the smokestack of Classic Warships *USS Miami* before gluing the stack onto the superstructure.

When painting photoetched railings, use masking tape to hold down the parts. When the paint is dry, flip the parts over to paint the undersides of the railings.

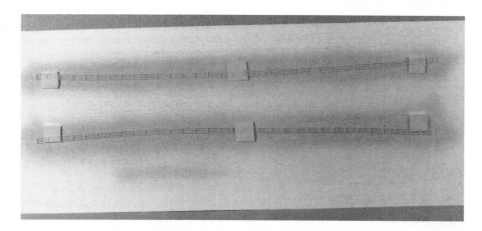

Paint long lengths of railings on their sides, especially railing lengths with bow curves. Use a minimal amount of tape when holding down these long parts, and be very careful when you flip them over. It's easy to distort the shape of these long railings, especially if the thickness of the photoetching is five thousandths (.005) of an inch or less.

Here is another example of working in subassemblies. Since both mast structures will be painted black, it made a lot of sense to attach the photoetched railings to the structures before gluing. This approach also eliminates any touchup work, which is normally necessary when you glue photoetched railings to painted surfaces.

Glue photoetched railings with super glue applied with a thin brass wire applicator. Dip the tip of the wire in super glue and run it across the base of the railing. Glue down the entire base of a railing length; otherwise the railing may bow. The glue will appear glossy when dry. To dull it, use a detail brush to paint the super glue with Testors Dullcote.

To help position 1/700 scale railings, you can use tweezers or a toothpick with a piece of masking tape attached to the tip.

When you're working on 1/350 scale ships, you will have to splice railing to achieve a continuous length. When splicing them, cut the railing stanchion on one length and position the bars onto the stanchion of the other railing length. Then apply a tiny amount of super glue to each bar.

On large complex superstructures it's a good idea to add railings and ladders as you build up the kit. Work from the inside areas towards the outside areas.

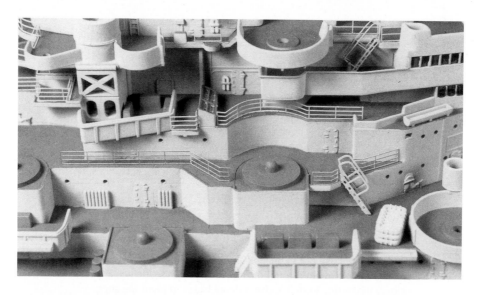

It's now time to install this railing. Just to be sure, give it one final fit check. Put the twin 5-inch mount in position as well to ensure that the railing does not come too close to the side of the gun mount.

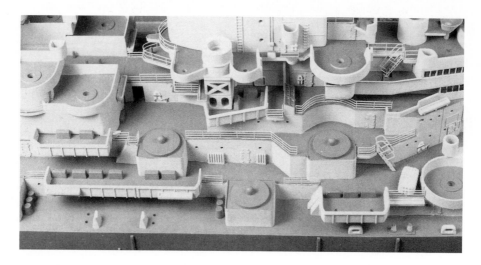

Install all the railings on the forward superstructure area on Tamiya's 1/350 scale *USS Missouri.* Now it's time to start adding the guns and other fittings.

The lower level railings on these kit parts need trimming because they interfere with the placement of the gun director.

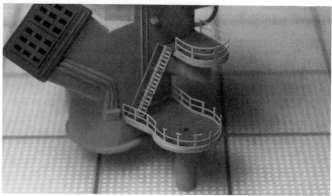

Carefully snip the crossbars and then cut off the upper stanchion lengths. A sharp set of small wire cutters does all the cutting.

Sand down the remaining stubs using a Flex-I-File sanding stick and repaint the surfaces. (I was lucky I caught this problem before the part was glued onto the superstructure, as it would have been ten times harder to fix it.)

Vertical ladders must have stubs on both ends to offset the ladder from the side of the superstructure.

It's easy to bend inclined ladders using two single-edge razor blades. Hold the part in place along the fold line with one edge, and slip the other under the part along the bend.

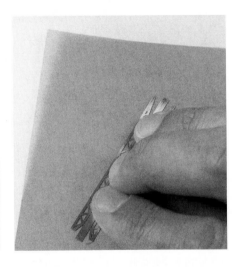

Here again, be sure to clean the surfaces and the gluing edges of photoetched parts. This is especially critical when photoetched parts are to be assembled.

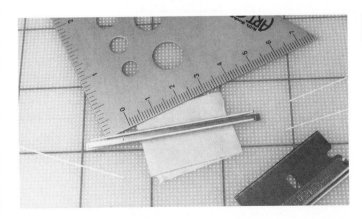

If a catapult has a separate photoetched surface, I like to reinforce the inside of the catapult with strip stock so there will be a larger gluing edge for the surface.

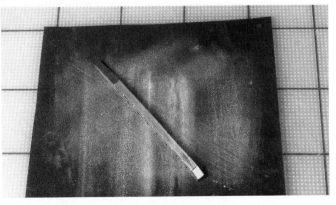

You can also use a stationary piece of sandpaper to clean super glue from the surfaces of photoetching.

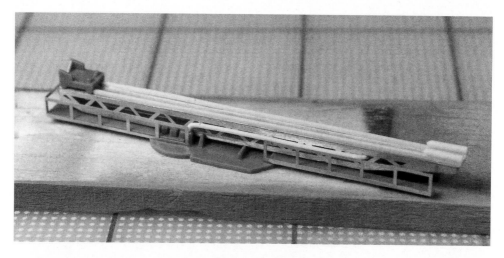

I built up this early Gold Medal Models catapult design with a combination of photoetched parts and kit parts.

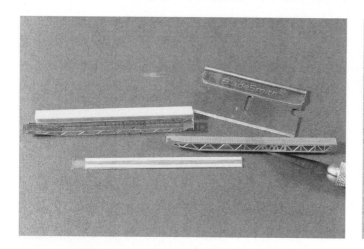

Newer photoetched designs have complete catapults that do not require the use of kit parts. Use Evergreen strip stock as an interior form to bend the sides of the photoetched catapult. Attach the reinforcing strips to the underside of the catapult top.

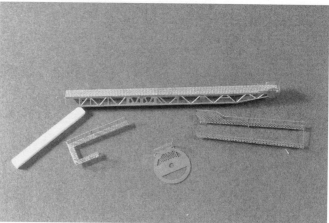

The subassemblies on this Gold Medal Models 1/350 scale catapult are now ready for final assembly.

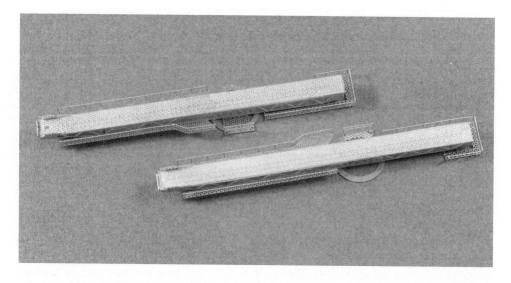

It is a good idea to build up sets of parts together. Then the chance is less that one completed assembly will be different from another.

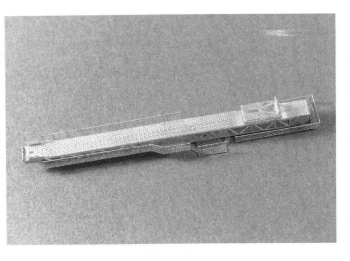

Here is the photoetched catapult complete with the aircraft stand. This part is now ready to be painted and installed.

A photoetched catapult for a resin ship kit. While not as accurate as the Gold Medal Models catapult designs, it is simpler to build.

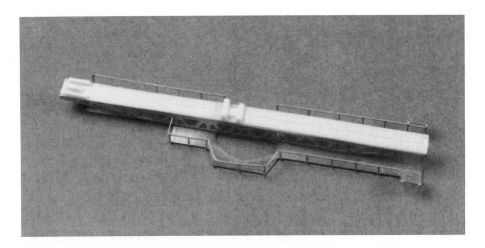

Instead of several photoetched parts, the surface of the catapult and all the detail are cast as one resin piece that fits into the top of the catapult frame.

Cranes can be a bit touchy to bend into shape. I fold the sides up on one side of the lower arm and both sides of the upper arm.

I then use two single-edge razor blades to carefully make the two interior folds. I bend along alternate fold lines until the crane is almost closed. Then I use a pair of tweezers to complete the enclosure.

With a Waldron punch tool you can make just about any size pulley you need to add detail to a crane.

This 1/350 scale Gold Medal Models crane is now complete. After painting and rigging, it will look great.

Here is the same crane painted, rigged, and installed.

You can also use a Waldron punch tool to hide tiny flaws or take care of fit problems between photoetched parts and kit-supplied parts.

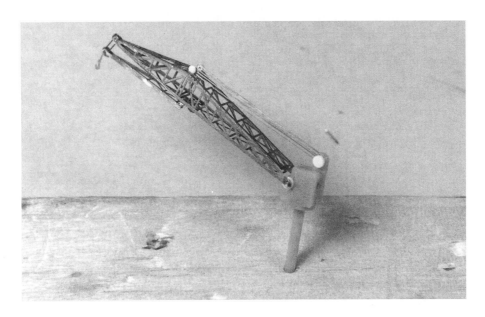

Several different-size disks have been attached to this completed 1/600 scale crane to cover flaws and help the photoetched part fit better.

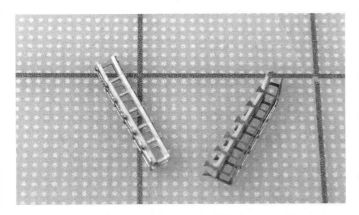

Photoetched depth charge racks can also be made stronger by gluing small lengths of Evergreen strip to the underside.

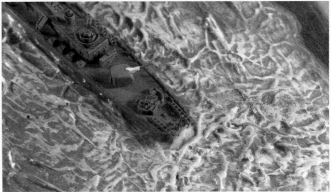

These 1/700 scale depth charge racks increase the level of detail and realism on this small kit. Working in small scale can be quite a challenge, but the end results are rewarding.

White-metal torpedo tubes can come as separate parts or as one casting. If the individual tubes are separate, be very careful when gluing them into place. If they are skewed, they will stand out like sore thumbs.

These K racks and hoists look great on this 1/350 scale MB Models *USS Gearing.* Note that all the racks look the same.

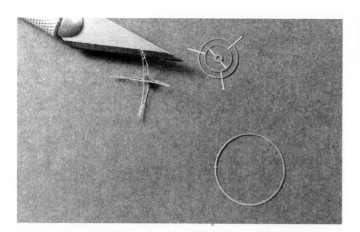

Photoetched radars can be a bit tricky to build up. Carefully remove and trim these subassemblies.

To assemble this SK-2 radar, I glued it together on a piece of wax paper. The super glue overspill tacked the part down to the wax paper, but the glue will not stick to the wax. I attached the cross piece first and then glued the V-shaped pieces into place.

Although photoetched parts were supplied for the base of the radar, I cut up the kit-supplied part and used it as the base.

Here is the completed radar sitting atop the main mast of Tamiya's 1/350 scale *Missouri*.

Photoetched MK-37 radars require some surgery to the MK-37 bases. Remove the cast parts from the top of the director and add photoetched frames.

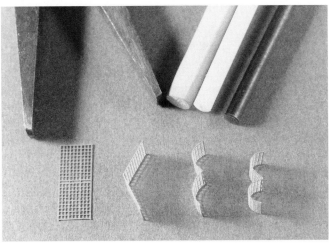

Bending the MK-37 radars is a three-step process. I use combinations of dowels and pliers.

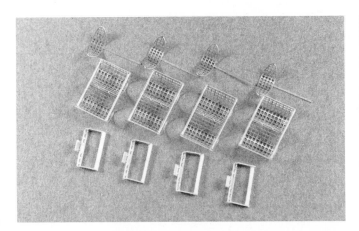

Here again, it is important to work in sets so that all the parts will be similar in appearance. The radar frames and the radars are now ready for final assembly. Add small lengths of Evergreen rod to the frames so that the radars will have a good gluing surface.

This is the final step in the assembly before painting. Paint the radars black, and the bases light gray.

Here is the completed MK-37 radar painted and installed. This is a Gold Medal Models design and it looks great.

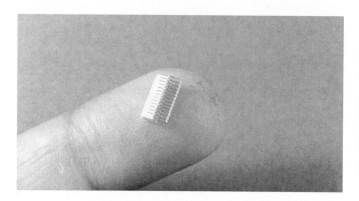

Enhance this MK-8 16-inch gun director radar with a small strip of Evergreen strip stock.

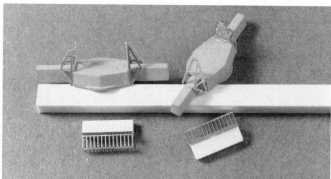

The subassemblies for both 16-inch gun directors are complete and ready for painting.

The complete 16-inch director. The photoetched version looks a lot more impressive than the stock kit parts.